Collins

Extended Essay
Student Handbook

Ashley Denham Busse and Michele Lackovic

for the IB Diploma Programme

William Collins' dream of knowledge for all began with the publication of his first book in 1819. A self-educated mill worker, he not only enriched millions of lives, but also founded a flourishing publishing house. Today, staying true to this spirit, Collins books are packed with inspiration, innovation and practical expertise. They place you at the centre of a world of possibility and give you exactly what you need to explore it.

Published by Collins
An imprint of HarperCollins*Publishers*
The News Building, 1 London Bridge Street, London, SE1 9GF, UK

HarperCollins*Publishers*
Macken House, 39/40 Mayor Street Upper, Dublin 1, D01 C9W8, Ireland

Browse the complete Collins catalogue at
collins.co.uk

© HarperCollins*Publishers* Limited 2025

10 9 8 7 6 5 4 3 2 1

A catalogue record for this publication is available from the British Library.

ISBN 978-0-00-877029-7

All rights reserved. No part of this publication may be reproduced, stored in a retrieval system, or transmitted in any form by any means, electronic, mechanical, photocopying, recording or otherwise, without the prior written permission of the Publisher or a licence permitting restricted copying in the United Kingdom issued by the Copyright Licensing Agency Ltd, 5th Floor, Shackleton House, 4 Battle Bridge Lane, London SE1 2HX.

Without limiting the exclusive rights of any author, contributor or the publisher of this publication, any unauthorised use of this publication to train generative artificial intelligence (AI) technologies is expressly prohibited. HarperCollins also exercise their rights under Article 4(3) of the Digital Single Market Directive 2019/790 and expressly reserve this publication from the text and data mining exception.

Authors: Ashley Denham Busse and Michele Lackovic
Publisher: Catherine Martin
Product developer: Daniela Mora Chavarría
Development editor: Sonya Newland
Copyeditor: Mark Gadd
Proofreader: Catherine Dakin
Cover designer: Amparo Barreras
Typesetter and illustrator: Six Red Marbles
Production controller: Alhady Ali
Printed and Bound in the UK by Martins the Printers Ltd.

This book contains FSC™ certified paper and other controlled sources to ensure responsible forest management.

For more information visit: www.harpercollins.co.uk/green
collins.co.uk/sustainability

Acknowledgements
With thanks to Abhinandan Bhattacharya at Finland International School, Race Course, Mumbai and Jill Meadow for their review comments.

The publishers gratefully acknowledge the permission granted to reproduce the copyright material in this book. Every effort has been made to trace copyright holders and to obtain their permission for the use of copyright material. The publishers will gladly receive any information enabling them to rectify any error or omission at the first opportunity.

We are grateful to the International Baccalaureate Organization for their permission to reproduce copyright material under licence, including the IB Learner Profile attributes, the Approaches to Learning skills, the Interdisciplinary frameworks, the Assessment Criteria, the IB Guidelines for the Extended Essay and the Guiding questions from the IB Extended Essay Guide © International Baccalaureate Organization, 2023.

This work has been developed independently from and is not endorsed by the International Baccalaureate Organization. International Baccalaureate, Baccalauréat International, Bachillerato Internacional and IB are registered trademarks owned by the International Baccalaureate Organization.

Contents

How to use this book 4

The IB learner profile 6

Approaches to learning skills 7

1. What is the extended essay? 8
2. Before you begin 12
3. The nature of research and the extended essay 22
4. Choosing and narrowing your topic 32
5. Understanding your selected IB subject(s) 43
6. Research methods and strategies 54
7. Planning and organising your essay 66
8. Citing and integrating sources 74
9. Structuring your essay 82
10. Writing your essay 94
11. Revising, editing and presenting your essay 108
12. Supervisor meetings and the reflective statement 116
13. The whole you: coming full circle 127

Glossary 129

How to use this book

This user-friendly student handbook has been designed to help support you through each stage of the extended essay process to allow you to tackle this challenge with confidence.

- Each chapter includes a **quick overview** of the main topics covered, to guide you through the structure:

> ### This chapter covers the following:
> - The research phase
> - Types of sources
> - Finding and evaluating sources
> - Using sources
> - Using AI tools in research
> - Organising your research materials

- The main learner profile **learner profile** traits featured are also highlighted at the forefront of each chapter:

> ### Learner profile traits
> Balanced
> Reflective
> Open-minded

- **Examples** showcase a range of subject areas and interdisciplinary topics and model different ways of approaching each stage of the process:

> ### Example
> Look at this research question:
>
> > 'To what extent was the Second World War ultimately good for American women?'
>
> The problem here is, what does 'good' mean in this context? On which aspects, elements, events or outcomes of the Second World War will the essay focus? Which aspects of American women's lives?
>
> A measurable research question might be:
>
> > 'To what extent did American women who held wartime industrial jobs during the Second World War maintain higher workforce participation rates and wages in the ten years immediately following the war?'
>
> This question establishes a clear **metric** and focus for measuring the 'goodness' of the war for American women: their continued employment and their compensation. It also meets the other criteria for a good research question.

- **Now you try it** tasks and **Activities** support reflection and prompt you to put your learning into practice, building evidence for the Reflective Statement:

> ### Activity
>
> **You might start by considering some of the following questions:**
>
> - What courses do I enjoy?
> - What am I interested in?
> - What jobs or fields of study am I considering for my future?
> - What is something I feel strongly about?
> - What is something I would like to know more about?
> - Has something happened (in the news or in my life) in recent years that I would like to learn more about?
> - Is there a topic or subject I have studied in one of my courses that I could learn more about?
> - What are my hobbies and interests, and how might I turn those into a topic for research and analysis?
> - What is a problem I see in the world?
> - Is there something I have learned about or already know, which I could approach from a different angle or *perspective*?
> - Is there a global idea or issue I might investigate at a more local or personal level, or vice versa?
> - Are there beliefs or assumptions about a topic that I might investigate or challenge?
> - Could I investigate the causes or effects of a topic I am interested in?
> - Is there a particular figure in my field of study whose work I could investigate to find ideas, or an author I enjoy reading?

> ### Now you try it
>
> Choose at least five of the questions in the activity above and brainstorm ideas. Use your Researcher's Reflection Space (RRS) to record your ideas. In addition to brainstorming on your own, consider chatting with a friend or teacher about possible ideas and avenues to explore.

- **Remember** boxes highlight essential points within each chapter:

> ### Remember
>
> Remember that the extended essay is a self-directed process, so that it is ultimately *your* responsibility, not your supervisor's, to know and understand the requirements of an extended essay in that subject(s). This is especially true if you choose an interdisciplinary pathway, as your supervisor may not be familiar with the requirements of a subject they do not teach.

- **Key takeaways** checklists summarise the learning in each chapter, for easy reference:

> ### Key takeaways: Chapter 6
>
> - Research is cyclical, not linear. Expect to revisit, rethink and refine your approach throughout the process.
> - The quality of your sources matters. Focus on academic sources such as peer-reviewed journals, and avoid unreliable sources like Wikipedia that cannot be verified.
> - Organisation is key! Keep systematic notes, folders and citation tracking from day one.
> - Engage actively. Do not just read sources, but evaluate, analyse and connect them to your research.
> - Use AI wisely, for search and organisation. Never use it for content generation or critical thinking.

- **Key terms** are bolded within the text and are defined at the end of the chapter as well as in the Glossary at the end of the book:

> ### Key terms
>
> **fieldwork:** investigations or search for material or data in a real, natural environment rather than in school, work or laboratory
>
> **informed consent:** permission given by someone who understands fully what they are agreeing to
>
> **parenthetical:** referring to something that is written or said in addition to the main part of what you are saying, or information found inside a set of parentheses such as an in-text citation

The IB learner profile

The IB learner profile consists of ten key characteristics that the International Baccalaureate designed to help you nurture and develop. These traits will help you become more well-rounded, empathetic, confident and self-aware, and equip you with valuable skills that extend well beyond the classroom.

The IB learner profile

The aim of all IB programmes is to develop internationally minded people who, recognising their common humanity and shared guardianship of the planet, help to create a better and more peaceful world.

IB learners strive to be:

Inquirers: We nurture our curiosity, developing skills for inquiry and research. We know how to learn independently and with others. We learn with enthusiasm and sustain our love of learning throughout life.

Knowledgeable: We develop and use conceptual understanding, exploring knowledge across a range of disciplines. We engage with issues and ideas that have local and global significance.

Thinkers: We use critical and creative thinking skills to analyse and take responsible action on complex problems. We exercise initiative in making reasoned, ethical decisions.

Communicators: We express ourselves confidently and creatively in more than one language and in many ways. We collaborate effectively, listening carefully to the perspectives of other individuals and groups.

Principled: We act with integrity and honesty, with a strong sense of fairness and justice, and with respect for the dignity and rights of people everywhere. We take responsibility for our actions and their consequences.

Open-minded: We critically appreciate our own cultures and personal histories, as well as the values and traditions of others. We seek and evaluate a range of points of view, and we are willing to grow from the experience.

Caring: We show empathy, compassion and respect. We have a commitment to service, and we act to make a positive difference in the lives of others and in the world around us.

Risk-takers: We approach uncertainty with forethought and determination; we work independently and cooperatively to explore new ideas and innovative strategies. We are resourceful and resilient in the face of challenges and change.

Balanced: We understand the importance of balancing different aspects of our lives – intellectual, physical, and emotional – to achieve well-being for ourselves and others. We recognise our interdependence with other people and with the world in which we live.

Reflective: We thoughtfully consider the world and our own ideas and experience. We work to understand our strengths and weaknesses in order to support our learning and personal development.

Approaches to learning skills

The IB approaches to learning help you build skills to become a better learner in all your IB classes. It focuses on five important skill areas – how you think, communicate, work with others, manage yourself, and conduct research. Instead of teaching these skills separately, your teachers work them into all your subjects. This creates a shared language across your classes and helps you become the kind of curious, knowledgeable and caring person the IB wants to develop. It also helps you understand your own learning style – not just what you are learning, but how you learn best. These are skills you will use long after school, in college and throughout your life.

Approaches to learning skills

Thinking skills: learn to question ideas, come up with creative solutions, use what you learn in one subject to help in another, and think about how you are learning

Social skills: learn how to work in teams, take the lead when needed, understand feelings (yours and others'), and resolve conflicts

Communication skills: get better and more confident at sharing your ideas, really listening to others, and understanding people from different cultures

Self-management skills: learn how to keep track of your work, use your time wisely, stay focused, recover from setbacks, and find study methods that work for you

Research skills: know how to find reliable information, understand media messages, use information responsibly, and do honest academic work

Chapter 1 – What is the extended essay?

This chapter covers the following:
- What is the extended essay?
- How is the extended essay assessed?
- How does the extended essay fit into the IB Diploma Programme?
- What are the extended essay pathways?

Learner profile traits
open-minded

What is the extended essay?

The extended essay is an in-depth, independent research project on a topic of your choice, culminating in a 4,000-word essay. However, this part of the course is not just about the final essay. Like all your IB Diploma Programme coursework, it is a journey during which you will develop skills that help you:

- plan and manage large projects
- research effectively
- think critically about complex topics
- express your ideas clearly
- work independently
- solve problems step by step.

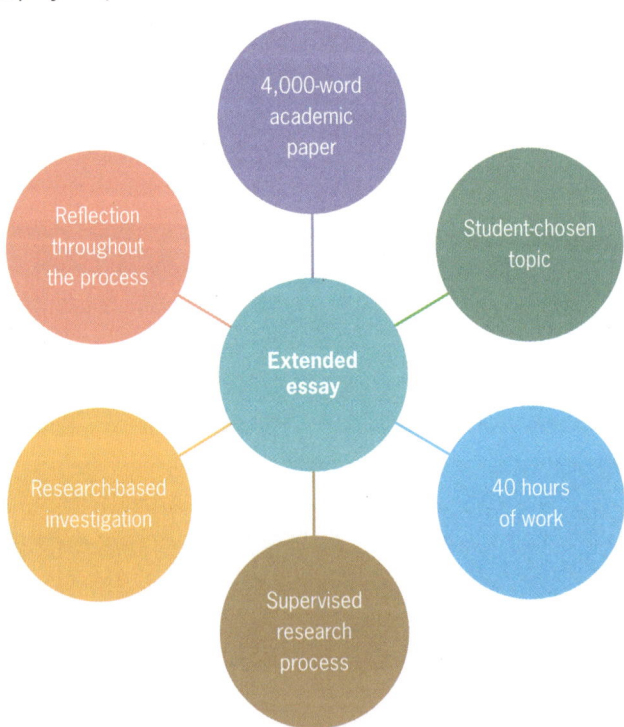

The essay is student-directed, and will be completed outside your regular Diploma Programme coursework. You should spend about 40 hours on it over the course of several months.

Your essay should incorporate **scholarly** research, which must be properly credited and **cited**. The topic you write about will be developed from one or two of your six IB Diploma Programme subjects, and you can choose one of two pathways:

- Subject-specific: a single IB DP subject focus
- **Interdisciplinary**: combining the methods, practices and **frameworks** of two subjects.

Throughout the process, you will be guided and mentored by a supervisor – usually an IB teacher. You will have about 3–5 hours of supervision time overall. The process also involves regular reflection and meetings with your supervisor, which are recorded in the Reflection and Progress Form (RPF) and assessed in Criterion E (see below).

How is the extended essay assessed?

The extended essay is assessed externally by IB examiners. It is scored on a scale of 1–30, according to five assessment criteria:

- Criterion A: Framework for the essay (research question, research methods, structure) (6 marks)
- Criterion B: Knowledge and understanding (6 marks)
- Criterion C: Analysis and line of argument (6 marks)
- Criterion D: Discussion and evaluation (8 marks)
- Criterion E: Reflection (growth and self-evaluation) (4 marks)

Your total marks out of 30 are then converted to a letter grade from A–E. D is the lowest passing grade.

How does the extended essay fit into the IB Diploma Programme?

The extended essay is a required component of the IB Diploma Programme. It must be completed and passed with a grade of D or higher in order for you to be eligible for the IB Diploma. The grade you receive for your extended essay is combined with your theory of knowledge (TOK) grade to earn you up to 3 points towards your IB Diploma, as shown below.

		Extended essay				
		A	B	C	D	E or N
Theory of knowledge	A	3	3	2	2	Failing
	B	3	2	2	1	Failing
	C	2	2	1	0	Failing
	D	2	1	0	0	Failing
	E or N	Failing	Failing	Failing	Failing	Failing

What are the extended essay pathways?

> **The extended essay pathways**
>
> You have a choice of two pathways for your extended essay.
> It can be based on a single Diploma Programme subject area (for example, Psychology)
> or you can integrate two subject areas (for example, Psychology and Global Politics).

Pathway 1: The interdisciplinary approach

An interdisciplinary extended essay combines two IB Diploma Programme subjects (or 'disciplines') to design and investigate a topic. This means that your research will bridge two subjects by integrating their unique knowledge, frameworks and research methods to explore a question that neither field could fully address on its own. By combining two subjects, the interdisciplinary approach allows you to develop a more comprehensive understanding of your chosen topic, and of those two subjects.

Pathway 2: The subject-focused approach

The subject-focused pathway offers the opportunity to really expand, deepen and strengthen your understanding of a Diploma Programme subject and a topic within that subject. The subject-focused pathway can increase your confidence and fluency in that subject, which will help prepare you for the examination in that subject.

Choosing a pathway

When choosing which approach to take, you should consider the benefits and challenges each might present. If you are particularly interested in and comfortable with one subject, you might want to follow the subject-focused pathway. If you select the interdisciplinary pathway, you should be studying at least one of the two subjects, and should be willing to learn about the concepts, **theories** and methods of the second subject if you have not already studied it. You should consider your own strengths and the time and attention you are able to give to the project. It is perfectly acceptable to opt for the single-subject approach if you are not confident about learning a new subject or about integrating two subjects.

There is more information about the different pathways in Chapter 4.

Learner profile traits and approaches to learning skills

The extended essay is a good opportunity to cultivate and strengthen the learner profile traits and approaches to learning skills that are key parts of the IB.

As you begin to brainstorm ideas for your essay, try to identify which of these skills and traits this part of the programme requires, and how you might cultivate them. For example:

- One of the purposes of the extended essay is to help you become more knowledgeable – not just about your chosen topic but about the world of scholarly research, the writing process and your own habits and practices as a learner, communicator and global citizen.

- Exploring possible topics in the brainstorming phase requires you to be open-minded about whether your topic would be best explored via one subject area or by combining approaches from two subjects. It also requires you to be flexible with your research question and the direction of your investigation.
- The extended essay itself is a process of ongoing inquiry in which you ask questions, seek solutions, and then ask new questions. You should remain open to new knowledge and experiences throughout the process.
- Struggling to understand the task and to determine a topic might be frustrating and tiring at times, so drawing on your own internal motivation and resilience, and other **self-management skills**, will be vital.

Key takeaways: Chapter 1

The extended essay:
- is a 4,000-word research essay on a topic of your choice from one or two IB DP subjects, completed with supervisor guidance
- requires approximately 40 hours of work over several months, outside of regular coursework
- is a mandatory component of the IB core curriculum that must be passed with grade D or higher
- can earn up to 3 bonus points towards your IB Diploma when combined with theory of knowledge (TOK) grade
- is assessed externally by IB examiners on 5 criteria using a 30-point scale (converted to A–E letter grades).

Key terms

cite: give credit to someone else's work

framework: the essential concepts, theories and approaches that underpin a subject of study

interdisciplinary: combining more than one academic subject to examine topics or solve problems

scholarly: work that is formal, sophisticated and methodical and usually involves research and critical thinking

self-management skills: skills that help you take control of your own learning, behaviour and processes, such as time management, motivation, making informed choices, and so on

theory: formal statement of ideas that explain an observation

Chapter 2 – Before you begin

This chapter covers the following:
- Understanding the 'Why'
- Recognising the importance of regular reflection
- Organising your time
- Maintaining balance

Learner profile traits
Knowledgeable
Thinkers
Balanced
Reflective
Communicators

The extended essay represents a significant academic undertaking, so it is important to get to grips with several key principles before you begin. These guidelines are integral to every phase of your extended essay journey – from generating initial ideas, through to the final submission, and beyond.

Understanding the 'Why'

One of the unique benefits of an IB education is its focus on the 'whole you' – that is, every part of who you are, not just your academic knowledge.

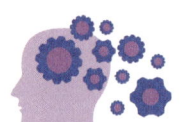
How you think and solve problems

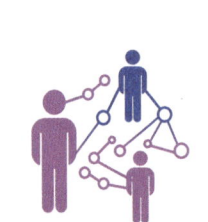
How you understand different cultures and perspectives

How you take care of your physical and mental health

How you connect with your community

How you express yourself clearly

In this way, the IB is more than just a series of academic courses, assignments, and deadlines leading to a final goal. Instead, you can think of it as a way of developing and exploring your identity, your values and passions, your gifts and areas for growth, both inside and outside of the classroom.

The IB journey helps you to cultivate important attributes and life skills. It instils habits of service, activity and creativity. It inspires curiosity and learning in a range of fields of study. And it helps you gain a deeper understanding of yourself and your place within the communities you belong to – from your friendship circles to your town and even the wider global society.

The 'whole you' wheel

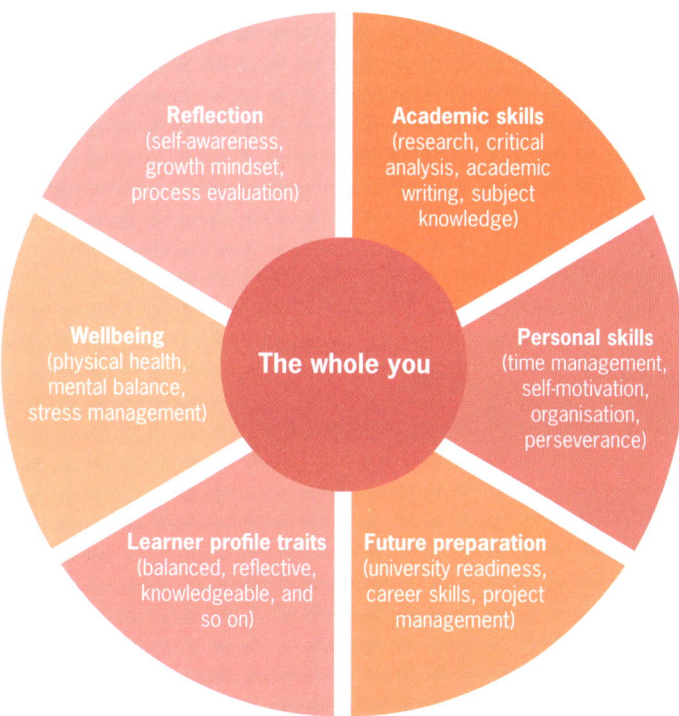

The extended essay and the rest of the IB Core

You may already have begun your theory of knowledge (TOK) course. Many IB students find that this changes the way they see themselves and the world in a fundamental way. That's because theory of knowledge invites you to step back, examine, reflect on and judge *how* you know what you know. But like the other IB Diploma Programme courses, theory of knowledge is not meant to stand alone. Rather, it helps you think more critically, creatively and open-mindedly about everything you are learning, both in school and in the wider world. The lessons learned in theory of knowledge are ones you will keep throughout your life, as they will help you question and test beliefs and understanding so that you 'own' that knowledge actively, rather than receiving it passively.

Like TOK, creativity, activity and service (CAS) is also designed to be part of life in and beyond the classroom. It will help you acquire lifelong habits of creative thinking and making, physical activity and wellness, as well as service to others. CAS is another component of the IB's focus on the 'whole you'. As you engage in these activities and think about what you have learned, you will discover how each type of experience benefits you. CAS also reminds you of the importance of regular, deliberate reflection to encourage your own development as a happy, productive human being!

This also ties in with many of the learner profile traits and approaches to learning skills of the IB Programme (see pages 6–7). The extended essay draws on the knowledge and thinking skills you will acquire through your courses of study, while helping you practise sophisticated habits that will set you up for life. These include finding balance, practising reflection, developing self-management and communication skills, and learning to advocate for yourself and to grow in confidence.

> ### Remember
> In many ways, the extended essay is where you will implement the skills and knowledge you are developing in TOK, CAS and your Diploma courses. You will use them to create an advanced, in-depth, academic essay that will bring you into the world of professional scholarship in your own right.

Recognising the importance of regular reflection

One of the requirements of the extended essay is a 500-word written reflective statement, which will be recorded in the Reflection and Progress Form (RPF). You will complete this at the end of the extended essay process, and it is assessed in Criterion E. However, keeping written reflections *throughout* the process will make writing your final reflection much easier, as it will provide you with concrete experiences and insights to draw from. You can find out more about the reflective statement in Chapter 12. Done regularly and deliberately, reflection can make the entire extended essay experience less stressful, more productive and efficient and, as a result, much more enjoyable!

What is reflection and why does it matter?

In simple terms, reflection means taking time to think with intention – about yourself, your thoughts, feelings, actions, experiences, and ways of learning – to gain deeper understanding and self-awareness. It helps you grow, improve, and become more efficient, confident, and self-aware. Without reflection, progress can be slow or even stagnant, no matter how much you continue doing something.

The reflection cycle

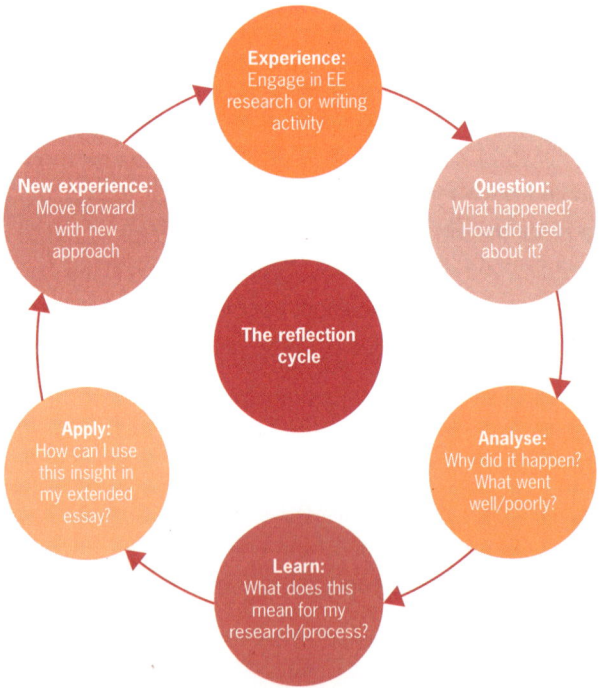

Example

Jian gave a presentation in his IB Economics class, but he did not feel good about it and did not receive the score he had hoped for. Instead of feeling upset about it, he took some time to reflect and use the experience to improve his next presentation.

Jian asked himself some reflective questions and made the following discoveries.

Question	Discovery
What happened? What went wrong?	I rushed through my presentation and ended up leaving out important talking points.
How was I feeling before and during the presentation, and why? Did that impact my performance?	I was stressed when putting together the presentation because I was running out of time. I was then nervous when delivering it because I had not given myself enough time to practise.
When I was preparing for the presentation, how did I spend my time and focus?	I should have started the project earlier because the research took longer than I thought and then I had other homework to do. I should have practised delivering the presentation a few times, rather than spending so long looking for images for my slides.
How will I use this experience to improve?	Next time I will start the project earlier instead of procrastinating. I will practise my delivery and time myself while I do it. I will find opportunities to practise speaking in front of people so that I am more comfortable.

It is also helpful to reflect on what *did* go well and what you feel good about. Identifying strengths is just as important as identifying any weaknesses. You can capitalise on your strengths and remind yourself of them when you need a confidence boost. After this presentation, Jian noted that he is knowledgeable about the content of his presentation and that his slides looked visually appealing. When planning for next time, he recognised that he should allow more time for graphic design, especially as that was a part of the process that he enjoyed.

The Researcher's Reflection Space

The IB recommends the use of a Researcher's Reflection Space (RRS) while you are writing the extended essay – a dedicated place to keep all useful materials. These might include:

- sources and research notes
- photos and videos
- your thoughts and reactions to what you are reading or examining
- your personal reflections at various points in the process
- generating ideas
- questions that arise
- reminders
- planning notes
- schedules and deadline-tracking
- notes from supervisor meetings.

The RRS is a great place to help you order your thinking, see your project unfold, and to reflect and plan for supervisor meetings. It is also an excellent portfolio to demonstrate and ensure academic integrity, as it will be a record of your process from brainstorming to final draft.

Throughout this book, activities and reflections ('Now you try it') have been suggested; completing them in your RRS is recommended.

> ### Remember
> The Researcher's Reflection Space can be digital, on paper, or both – use the format that works best for you. Your school may have a management system for uploading coursework and tracking CAS, which may have a digital space for your reflections. If not, you can set up your own RRS.

Practising reflection

While researching and writing your extended essay, you will find there are two major areas for reflection:

Content and findings

- what you are discovering about your topic
- how your understanding of the subject(s) is growing through reading and research
- where you might need additional research or thinking
- how your argument or analysis is developing

Your process and skills

- how you plan and organise your time
- which methods work best for you at each stage
- when you need to adjust your schedule
- what challenges you face and how you overcome them
- which strategies help you work most productively

Your reflections will be most useful if you consider both aspects each time.

> ### Activity
> Here are some questions you might ask yourself as part of your reflection:
>
> - What has happened since my last reflection? What have I done and not done?
> - What challenges or obstacles have I experienced and how did I feel about them? How do I feel about them now?
> - What do I feel good about? (This can be anything – something you have learned or discovered, something you have written or an idea you have had, or simply feeling proud of your time management or of your self-advocacy in asking for help.)
> - Where do I think I can improve?
> - What is my next concrete, achievable goal? ('In the next two weeks, I want/need to …')
> - What am I learning about myself in terms of my time management, communication, organisation and research skills?

- How is my thinking about my topic changing?
- Are there any barriers I need to overcome to proceed?
- Do I need to rethink or revise my topic, research question or research focus?
- Have I seen connections to my extended essay in other areas of my IB Diploma programme or in real life?
- Has any aspect of the extended essay process helped me improve in another area of life or study?
- Do I need to ask someone for help?
- Am I keeping to my schedule? What adjustments might I need to make?

Now you try it

In your RRS or a journal, write today's date. Then take a couple of minutes to sit quietly, with no expectation of doing or thinking anything. You might focus on your breathing or practise relaxation exercises.

Now, reflect on the following questions, noting down your responses in a way that works for you:

- Who am I – how would I define myself to the world?
- What do I care about?
- What has my CAS experience taught me about myself so far?
- Which learner profile trait describes me already, and why/how?
- Which learner profile trait do I want to develop or strengthen? If this trait is not something that comes naturally to me, why is that? How might I challenge myself to develop this trait, both in school and outside?
- How do I feel about the extended essay? What questions or concerns do I have? How might I resolve them?

Make a plan to review this reflection in a week or two to see how your feelings and thoughts have changed.

Create a schedule for these reflections – for example, once every two weeks. That might seem like a lot, but remember that reflection is self-care. It helps you:

- catch problems early, before they become overwhelming
- break down a big project into manageable pieces
- stay focused on your goals
- reduce stress by tracking your progress
- know when to ask for help.

Organising your time

The extended essay is student-driven, which means that although you have a supervisor to guide you, ultimately you are working independently. Your school may give you some broader deadlines to meet, but this is a long-term project, so you should set yourself interim deadlines to keep everything on track. Make sure you ask your supervisor for guidance in between formal meetings if necessary. Be proactive and resourceful.

Activity

Step 1: Take a moment to answer these questions honestly:

- How many hours a week do you realistically have available to devote to your extended essay?
- What are your biggest time constraints (extracurricular activities, other IB coursework, family commitments, job, and so on)?
- When do you typically procrastinate and why?
- What time of day are you most productive and focused?

Step 2: Get a calendar that shows all the months until the final deadline for your extended essay. Mark these key dates:

- Final extended essay submission deadline
- First draft deadline
- Check-in meetings with your supervisor
- Any known busy periods (such as exams, holidays, family events)

Working backwards from the final deadline, split the schedule into the following key phases (or the deadlines or milestones your school has created):

- Phase 1: Topic selection and research question formulation
- Phase 2: Initial research and creating an outline
- Phase 3: Detailed research and note-taking
- Phase 4: Writing first draft
- Phase 5: Revisions based on supervisor feedback
- Phase 6: Final editing and formatting

Assign realistic timeframes to each phase (for example, Phase 1: 3 weeks, Phase 2: 4 weeks).

Step 3: Create a template for your weekly extended essay work schedule.

- Identify 2–3 specific time blocks each week (1–2 hours each) dedicated to extended essay work.
- For the upcoming week, assign specific tasks to each time block (for example, 'Monday 4–6 p.m.: Research sources for section 1').
- Include one 'buffer' session each week for unexpected delays or additional work.

Step 4: Identify three potential obstacles to maintaining your schedule and write down one strategy to overcome each. For example:

- Obstacle: Getting distracted by social media during research sessions.
- Strategy: Use website blockers during dedicated extended essay time blocks and set phone to 'Do Not Disturb'.

Next steps:

- Share your schedule with your supervisor for feedback.
- Set up regular check-ins with yourself to evaluate your progress.
- Be prepared to adjust your schedule as needed, but maintain consistent weekly work.
- Use a tracking system (digital or paper) to monitor your progress.

Now you try it

Use your RRS and any planning or calendar tools you have, and create your own schedule based on realistic, achievable checkpoints and deadlines.

Remember

By creating and following an extended essay schedule, you will:

- reduce stress by breaking a large project into manageable chunks
- ensure adequate time for supervisor feedback and revisions
- produce higher-quality work through consistent effort rather than rushed completion
- develop valuable time management skills that will benefit you in university and beyond
- create balance with other IB components and personal activities.

RRS Organisation system

| Research notes (annotated notes, questions, highlighted text) | Planning and timeline (calendar, deadlines, checklists) | Reflections (journal entries, thought bubbles, mind maps) | Sources and bibliography (organised source list, citations, ratings) | Ideas and brainstorming (mind maps, free writing, diagrams) | Notes from supervisor meetings. |

Remember

There are many digital applications available online which can help by sending reminders for the deadlines you have set. There are even free apps that give you 'rewards' as you meet requirements. A quick internet search can help you locate these types of services.

Timing and scheduling

When creating deadlines and schedules remember that most tasks will take longer than you think. People tend to be optimistic when planning and they forget that challenges occur! Consider doubling the amount of time you believe a task will take. If possible, speak to a student who has already completed their extended essay and ask them to share their experiences.

Work backward from your major deadlines. As you do so, keep in mind the following considerations:

- The methods and practices of your chosen subject(s) and the time and materials they may require. For example, if you are conducting your own experiment (such as in Physics or Chemistry), remember to allow adequate time for:
  - obtaining required permissions forms
  - arranging supervision by a teacher with appropriate equipment

- gathering necessary supplies
- conducting the experiment
- gathering data.
- How much time you will need to complete certain tasks. For example, if you are writing your extended essay on longer literary or non-literary works, be sure to allow yourself time to read those **primary sources** at least once, annotating them as you read.

Maintaining balance

Creating and adhering to a schedule is one of the best ways to ensure you maintain balance during the process. So is allowing some flexibility in your schedule for the inevitable interruptions!

Here are some tips for maintaining balance:

- If possible, create a dedicated workspace to keep all your materials organised in one place.
- Use your CAS activities as they are intended: physical exercise or stretching are helpful; engaging in community service can give your brain a break and often lead to new insights, as can creative activity.
- Seek support and encouragement from your supervisor or other trusted adult, and consider forming a 'study group' in which you and some peers encourage each other and hold each other accountable for meeting your deadlines. Social connection can boost your mood.
- Schedule your extended essay work at times of day or night you know to be your best. Do not try to fight against your body's natural rhythms.
- Celebrate small achievements, such as meeting a self-imposed deadline or overcoming an obstacle.
- Cultivate a positive mindset. Use your reflection times to focus not just on what you need to do but on what you have done, what you are doing well, and how you are growing and improving.
- When you encounter setbacks or obstacles, train yourself to see them as opportunities, not obstructions.
- Set clear boundaries between work and rest time. While you are working, remove distractions such as mobile phones, but also take short breaks at regular intervals.
- Schedule your extended essay realistically around other commitments, rather than trying to squeeze it in late at night when you are tired or right at the last minute.
- Collect and surround yourself with photos or quotes that you find encouraging, positive and motivating. Look at them when you need a little boost!
- Remember: Taking care of your physical and mental health is not a 'break' from your work; it is a vital part of doing your best work. Rest and recreation are just as productive.

Key takeaways: Chapter 2

- The extended essay is an essential part of the IB Programme and seeks to nurture, develop and inspire the 'whole you'.
- Regular, written reflection is vital to the success of your extended essay; it also improves your knowledge and makes you more resilient and more self-aware.
- Managing and organising your time will reduce stress and lead to better, more efficient work during the extended essay process.
- It is important to maintain a healthy balance of work and rest as you journey through the extended essay.

Key term

primary source: original first-hand material of research, offering direct evidence without interpretation or analysis

Chapter 3 – The nature of research and the extended essay

This chapter covers the following:
- What is scholarly research?
- What makes a good research question, and why does it matter?
- The recursive nature of research

Learner profile traits
Open-minded
Inquirers
Knowledgeable
Thinkers
Balanced
Reflective

What is scholarly research?

Scholarly research is organised, intentional, methodical investigation into a question or issue. Through study, reading, experimentation, data collection and **analysis** – as well as *your* assessment and integration of others' research – you will reach new knowledge and understanding.

You will need to engage in scholarly research at some point in many of your IB Diploma subjects. The extended essay provides you with the opportunity to explore a topic of *your* choice in greater depth and over an extended period. You will become more familiar with how scholarly research is done in your topic's field(s) and become part of the ongoing scholarly conversation on that topic – becoming an expert in your own right.

Engaging in scholarly research will help to develop the 'whole you' and set you up for success in the next steps of your study or work. Completing a project like the extended essay sets you apart from your peers in other programmes of study, and it helps you develop the skills that universities and employers value. These include:

- problem-solving (often in creative ways)
- **critical thinking** (about others' research, claims, beliefs)
- analysis (understanding how knowledge and meaning are constructed)
- project and time management
- confidence in approaching larger, long-term projects
- knowledge of a topic you care about
- writing, editing and verbal communication
- the ability to balance multiple demands
- awareness of multiple perspectives and an ability to contribute to **public discourse** in a meaningful, informed way.

What makes a good research question, and why does it matter?

A good research question is the foundation of your entire project – not just the final essay, but the entire process. It provides a clear focus, guiding your work and laying the groundwork for in-depth discussion and analysis.

To create a good research question, you need to:

- think deeply and broadly about your topic; do preliminary brainstorming, research, rethinking, conversation (with peers, teachers and your supervisor) and reflection before settling on a topic
- use the clearest, most succinct and effective word choice in your question; this will keep your research and thinking clear, organised and efficient.

You will begin exploring topics and potential research questions in Chapter 4, but before you get there, it is important to understand the elements of a good research question.

Clear

Every word matters – not just for your reader's sake but also for your own. Clarity of language corresponds to clarity of thought, and vice versa. If you use vague or ambiguous words in your research question, you are setting yourself up for frustration in research (since search terms matter) and imprecision in your discussion (which may prevent you from reaching a clear conclusion).

At first it might be difficult to find words to express what you want to discuss, so give yourself time to:

- write – and rewrite – your question
- explore **synonyms** and related words
- look up definitions
- identify the terms and concepts used by scholars in the subject(s) you are exploring.

Thinking carefully about your language choices will help you to clarify, refine and strengthen your thinking, which will set you on the path to success.

Example

To begin with, it is important to find the word that most accurately represents what you mean. For example, here is a range of words that all mean the same as 'happiness' according to the dictionary:

- glee
- bliss
- delight
- pleasure
- contentment
- joy
- exhilaration
- ecstasy
- gladness
- cheerfulness

But if you think carefully about each of those words, you should recognise that they all have different **connotations**, shades of meaning and associations. So, in some **contexts**, 'exhilaration' might not communicate the kind of happiness you are thinking of; 'contentment' might be a better fit. Taking the time to determine the most accurate and specific word will force you to think more carefully about what exactly you want to communicate with that word. It will also ensure that your discussion, **evaluation** and analysis are concrete and specific.

Consider the following scenario: José wants to write a Psychology extended essay, and is interested in this question: 'What is the impact of social media on teens' happiness and well-being?'

This topic is a great one to start with, but José will need to think carefully about a few of the words in this question. First, consider 'happiness' and 'well-being' as examples. As you have seen, 'happiness' can suggest a range of different states of mind. In a similar way, if you asked three people what they think of when they hear the term 'well-being', you might get three different (but equally valid) definitions. José needs to narrow and clarify his definition of these two terms *in his own mind*, to identify what sorts of psychological studies he will need to look for in his research. For example, will they be about emotional stability or physical health? Does happiness mean contentment, a lack of stress, or something else?

As he begins his background reading and preliminary research, José should also pay close attention to the terms and types of evidence scholars and practitioners in the field use when discussing what others might just call happiness and well-being. By tuning into the language and vocabulary used in your chosen subject, you can adopt similar words and phrases in your future searches.

Focused

The extended essay should be about 4,000 words. When you first start planning it, you may feel you have to select a broad topic so that you have enough to say. However, once you incorporate the required elements of scholarly research papers – such as a **methodology**, literature review, and **primary** and **secondary sources** – you may find that your topic is too broad, which will make your task more difficult. You might end up providing a wide range of material, but not enough depth, so you will be unable to demonstrate your critical thinking and analysis skills.

Example

Blake is interested in feminist movements of the twentieth century and how they were expressed in popular literature. This is a good, broad topic area to start with, but Blake will need to do some brainstorming, thinking and background reading to narrow these elements:

- Feminism: This is a very broad term and has been characterised by multiple movements within its larger context (first-wave feminism, second-wave feminism, and so on), so Blake has many options here: she can narrow her focus to one particular 'wave' or to one or two feminist concerns, such as economic independence, equality in marriage or oppressive beauty standards.
- Twentieth century: A century is a long time – too long to consider in an essay of this length. Blake's research will be easier to manage if she limits herself to a single generation or to a fixed period such as the 'Roaring Twenties'.
- Location: Blake has not specified a geographical location, but will need to do so, as feminism, history and literature vary across regions, nations and cultures.
- Popular literature: This, too, is a very broad term and so her research will lose focus. Once she has narrowed her location and period, she needs to define what she means by 'popular literature' and then narrow further to a particular literary form, such as novels, and then even further, to one or two novels representative of her larger idea.

As Blake starts to narrow her focus, she might also realise that what she is most interested in is a particular novel, or a type of poetry, or women's magazines. In addition, she might chat with a friend or a teacher who can ask her probing questions such as: 'Why are you interested in this topic?', 'What – in particular – about feminism interests you?', 'Why does this matter?', 'Why is literature a point of interest?' These questions may lead her to a different topic than the one she originally thought she was interested in – and that is fine!

Analytical

This component might be the most important for your research question – and the whole process – as analysis, evaluation and critical discussion form the core of good research and academic writing. So, what exactly is analysis, and how do you ensure you are doing it properly? To answer these questions, it is helpful to define some terms and discuss what analysis is *not*.

Analysis is …	Analysis is not …
• discussion of causes and effects • identifying patterns and relationships between events, facts, data, sources, texts and ideas • identifying advantages and disadvantages • evaluating strengths and weaknesses of sources, materials and your own writing • dissecting and interpreting research findings, concepts and ideas.	• a summary or description of facts • background information • the when or where • a research report • a narrative or **expository**

Summary, reporting and description tell what something is, what occurred or what it is about. In contrast, analysis explains what it means, how it is put together, why it matters and how it works. The 'it' here might be a literary work, a machine, a problem, an event, a system, a **theory** or a **hypothesis** to test. This is why, when crafting your research question, you should use command terms and question stems such as 'To what extent …?' or 'How and why …?' rather than questions that lead you to reporting or describing. The following table shows some examples of description versus analysis:

Description (what)	Analysis (why/how/so what)
The population decreased by 36%	The 36% population decrease suggests economic migration triggered by resource scarcity
The author uses metaphors throughout the poem	The water metaphors create a sense of inevitable destruction that undermines the poem's hopeful tone
The experiment showed a correlation	The correlation indicates a possible causal relationship due to …

Realistic

Just like a focused research question, a realistic one will ensure that you do not overestimate or underestimate the scope of the project. To be sure that you are setting yourself up for success, ask yourself these questions:

- Will I be able to locate, read and use an adequate number of both primary data and secondary sources for my topic?
  (Sometimes you can come up with a wonderful topic but there is little to no scholarly research available on it, or there are resources, but you do not have access to them.)
- Will I be able to do the above within the timeframe allotted for my extended essay (6–12 months)?
  (You might have a great idea but would need to perform a time-consuming experiment for it, or an experiment that would need too many resources, or one which would raise ethical or environmental concerns. Or you want to analyse long literary works but do not have time in your academic schedule to read and reread such long works.)
- Is my topic narrow enough to be addressed fully and thoroughly in 4,000 words?
  (You may have an amazing idea, but the topic would require several volumes of writing in order to be adequately addressed!)

Measurable

Think through the words and ideas in your research question so you are sure that they actually can be quantified or clearly observed and determined. In the example of José's Psychology essay, the word 'happiness' is very broad and has many possible meanings, but it is also difficult to measure in a reliable, scientific way. Even for an extended essay on literature, a discussion of a character's 'happiness' would need defining and clarifying. Non-measurable terms can cause several issues:

- They rely on opinion or are subjective rather than objective. (For example: What is happiness? Does that term fit all occasions? Who defines happiness?)
- They make it difficult to gather credible evidence. (For example: What system are you using to measure happiness?)
- Their 'results' cannot be reproduced in future investigations.
- They result in a vague, unfocused analysis.
- They make it difficult to maintain a clear, concrete focus on the desired outcome.

Example

Look at this research question:

'To what extent was the Second World War ultimately good for American women?'

The problem here is, what does 'good' mean in this context? On which aspects, elements, events or outcomes of the Second World War will the essay focus? Which aspects of American women's lives?

A measurable research question might be:

'To what extent did American women who held wartime industrial jobs during the Second World War maintain higher workforce participation rates and wages in the ten years immediately following the war?'

This question establishes a clear **metric** and focus for measuring the 'goodness' of the war for American women: their continued employment and their compensation. It also meets the other criteria for a good research question.

Relevant

One common error students make when deciding on an extended essay topic is not reading the subject-specific guidance. Many topics may seem to fall naturally into a category such as History or Literature, but the only way to be sure is to carefully read the subject guide(s). If you do not have these already, ask your supervisor to share them with you.

Subject-specific information also matters because there are some rules related to extended essays in certain subject areas. For example, a Language A extended essay must include a literary or language text originally written in the language in which the essay is written (that is, you cannot write on one or two translated works alone). In addition, Language A extended essays should mainly be focused on the chosen text(s) or **artefacts** rather than a cultural or social phenomenon of which the texts are merely representative. In other words, you may discuss the idea of the mental trauma of war as seen in *The Things They Carried* by Tim O'Brien (1990) and *The Sorrow of War* by Bao Ninh (1987), but an essay primarily about war's impact on mental health – even with some reference to the two novels – could not be the basis for a Language A extended essay. Instead, you would need to focus on how both novels, authors suggest, through various choices and literary techniques, that the horrors of war cause extreme mental trauma.

For interdisciplinary extended essays (see Chapter 1), you should be aware of subject-specific guidance for your selected subjects, but you should also ensure that the two subjects you have chosen are the best ones to address your question. For example, if you are interested in Visual Arts and Psychology, you may want to investigate how listening to different types of music can influence a person's perception of a painting. However, you will need to be comfortable with the frameworks and theories of both Visual Arts and Psychology. And, since psychological experiments are not permitted for the IB extended essay, you will need to determine how to approach the topic using existing scholarly research on the overlap between the creative and cognitive processes. Your supervisor will be able to help you with issues like this.

> ## Remember
> The extended essay may be your first piece of sustained, research-based writing. Many of your IB subjects require you to write research-informed essays, but none is 4,000 words. However, the research and writing process are largely the same, whether the piece of writing is a laboratory report, a literary analysis essay or a Philosophy internal assessment.

The recursive nature of research

There are two key truths about the research and writing process in general, and when you embrace these lessons, you will be able to tackle such projects with confidence.

Key truth 1

The first lesson – which requires you to be open-minded – is that YOU CAN DO THIS! Regardless of which subject and topic you choose, you can be a scholar in your own right, and you can contribute to the field you are studying. Of course, you have not completed an advanced degree in your chosen subject or subjects, and you may be more limited in terms of time and resources than professionals in the field. However, you have the intellectual ability to undertake a project of this length, complexity and magnitude. Everything you have been doing in your IB Diploma Programme subject coursework – from course content, readings and discussions to the assignments and assessments you have been given – helps cultivate your research, thinking, speaking and writing skills. Again, many of your internal and external assessments are smaller versions of the extended essay, so you already have done (or soon will do) similar work.

Key truth 2

Scholarly research and the writing process are both **recursive** (you may also hear them called 'iterative'). This means that these processes are not linear and may progress in ways you had not anticipated. Because the research and writing processes are often unpredictable and messy, it is very important to allow time for this 'chaotic' process. Quality thinking, research and writing will almost always take longer than you think, and they may cause frustration if you feel stuck or confused or are having difficulty locating resources you need. Remember to create a schedule that includes breaks for activity, fun and rest (see Chapter 2). Sticking to your schedule will help you maintain balance, which will make the process much more enjoyable!

> **Remember**
> Since the research and writing processes can be separate but are combined into one process for the extended essay, they will be referred throughout this book as a single process.

While the research process is recursive and messy, your journey will be guided by a strong research question. Understanding what makes an effective research question is fundamental to successful scholarly research. Before you develop your own research question in Chapter 4, complete the activity below to practise recognising and crafting strong research questions in general.

The research process

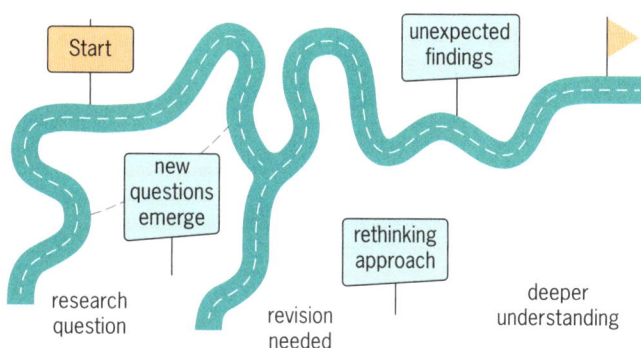

Activity

Now that you understand what makes scholarly research effective and how research involves a recursive process, try identifying the qualities of strong research questions that can guide this journey.

Part 1: Identify strong and weak research questions

Read each of the research questions below. For each one, determine whether it is a strong or weak research question for an extended essay. If you think it is weak, identify what issues make it problematic using the features discussed previously: clear, focused, analytical, realistic, measurable and relevant.

- How did the Second World War affect society?
- To what extent did the implementation of the Green Revolution in India between 1965 and 1975 increase agricultural productivity and worsen social inequality?
- Why is climate change bad?
- Does listening to classical music while studying improve test performance in high school students?
- How and why did Jean Rhys use Caribbean settings and characters to challenge colonial narratives in her novels written between 1930 and 1940?
- What are the different types of renewable energy?
- To what extent does Julia Alvarez's novel *In the Time of the Butterflies* (1994) accurately portray the Mirabal sisters' resistance against Trujillo's dictatorship?
- How beautiful is Impressionist art?

Part 2: Transforming weak research questions

Choose two of the weak research questions from Part 1 and transform them into strong research questions. Make sure your revised questions are clear, focused, analytical, realistic, measurable and relevant.

Now you try it

As you develop your understanding of scholarly research, practise crafting research questions using command terms that promote critical thinking. For each of the topics below, create a strong research question using one of the following command terms:

(To what extent) (How effectively) (How and why) (Compare and contrast) (Evaluate) (Analyse)

Choose three topics from this list:

- The representation of women in twenty-first century superhero films
- The effectiveness of microfinance in reducing poverty in Bangladesh
- The influence of social media on political polarisation
- The environmental impact of fast fashion
- Artificial intelligence in medical diagnostics

For each topic you choose, write a research question in your RRS that demonstrates your understanding of effective question formulation. Consider how your chosen command term encourages analysis rather than mere description.

Key takeaways: Chapter 3

- Scholarly research is systematic investigation through study, experimentation and analysis to create new knowledge and understanding.
- A good research question will make the entire extended essay process easier, more efficient and more successful.
- A good research question should be clear, analytical, realistic, measurable and relevant.
- The research and writing process is recursive and often messy – and that is normal!

Key terms

analysis: the process of considering something carefully or using statistical methods to understand or explain it

artefact: an object made by human work

connotation: an association or idea suggested by a word or phrase

context: the parts of a piece of writing, speech, and so on, that precede and follow a word or passage and contribute to its full meaning; the circumstances in which something occurs or exists

critical thinking: analysing and evaluating information to make sound judgements and informed decisions

evaluation: the process of assessing or judging the quality or importance of something

expository: a piece of writing that offers an explanation or narration of something

hypothesis: a suggested explanation for a group of facts or phenomena, which is accepted as likely to be true

methodology: the research approaches, frameworks, and strategies used in a particular discipline

metric: a standard for measuring or assessing something

primary source: an original, first-hand or contemporary account of an event or subject

public discourse: the formal or informal exchange of ideas and arguments on issues that affect society, often in public forums, such as media and debates

recursive: cyclical (rather than linear) structure, in which you return to different stages of the task (such as researching or writing) throughout the process

secondary source: a source that gives information about or analysis of a primary source, created by someone who did not experience an event first-hand

synonym: a word or expression that means the same as another word or expression

theory: a formal statement of ideas that explains an observation

Chapter 4 – Choosing and narrowing your topic

This chapter covers the following:
- Brainstorming ideas
- Narrowing your topic
- Responsible AI use in your research
- Deciding on a pathway

Learner profile traits
Caring
Reflective
Thinkers
Inquirers
Principled

There are several ways to arrive at a topic for your extended essay. This chapter offers a few exercises and activities to help you determine your interests, choose your subject(s) and start considering a research question.

Brainstorming ideas

There are several key factors to consider when you start thinking about a topic for your essay.

- It should be something that you care about. The extended essay involves months of research, writing and reflection, so it is important to focus on a topic that really interests you – something that you want to investigate for an extended period.
- It should lend itself to analysis and argument. The greater part of your essay will involve critically investigating the material you find, analysing and evaluating it, and integrating it with your own thinking to offer some new knowledge, theory or argument.
- It should fall within one or two IB Diploma subjects, at least one of which you are already enrolled in. Several elements of the assessment criteria evaluate how well your topic relates to the frameworks, theories and methods of the Diploma Programme subjects. Already being familiar with the approaches, terminology and concepts in at least one of the subjects will ensure that you use them appropriately and effectively to answer your research question. Indeed, one of the main aims of the extended essay task is to support, enhance and extend the learning you are already doing in those courses, so take advantage of that!

Remember

As an inquirer, there may be topics which you would like to learn more about, but you should make sure that your question does not simply lead to fact-finding or information-gathering. Instead, the information you learn, the **data** you collect and the material you read should just be the start.

Activity

You might start by considering some of the following questions:

- What courses do I enjoy?
- What am I interested in?
- What jobs or fields of study am I considering for my future?
- What is something I feel strongly about?
- What is something I would like to know more about?
- Has something happened (in the news or in my life) in recent years that I would like to learn more about?
- Is there a topic or subject I have studied in one of my courses that I could learn more about?
- What are my hobbies and interests, and how might I turn those into a topic for research and analysis?
- What is a problem I see in the world?
- Is there something I have learned about or already know, which I could approach from a different angle or **perspective**?
- Is there a global idea or issue I might investigate at a more local or personal level, or vice versa?
- Are there beliefs or assumptions about a topic that I might investigate or challenge?
- Could I investigate the causes or effects of a topic I am interested in?
- Is there a particular figure in my field of study whose work I could investigate to find ideas, or an author I enjoy reading?

Now you try it

Choose at least five of the questions in the activity above and brainstorm ideas. Use your Researcher's Reflection Space (RRS) to record your ideas. In addition to brainstorming on your own, consider chatting with a friend or teacher about possible ideas and avenues to explore.

Activity

When deciding on potential topics for your essay, it can be helpful to do some free-association **mind-mapping**. This exercise is a sort of free writing in a graphic format, and while much of what you write may seem nonsensical, by the end, you may identify some valuable points.

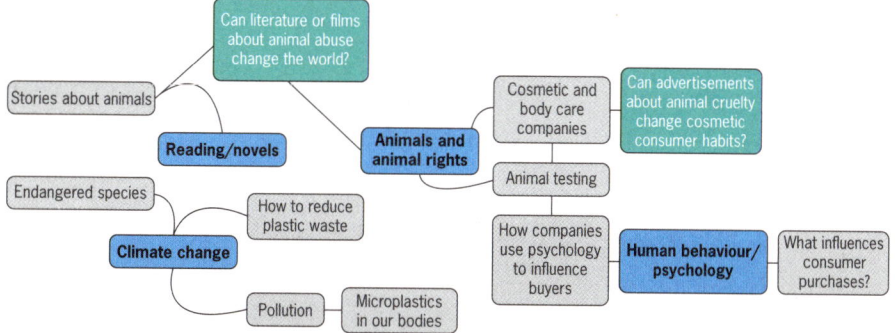

Now you try it

Note down 4–6 words or phrases that come to mind when you think of your interests or the subjects you are studying. Each time you write a word or phrase, draw a circle or box around it, leaving space around each one. Then, create smaller circles or boxes that branch out from each word or phrase; in those, put words and ideas that come to mind when you see the original word or phrase. When you reach the end, begin a new mind map with these new key words as your central boxes or circles. Keep doing this until you see a pattern of interests or ideas. Use this pattern to start brainstorming researchable topics.

Subject-specific brainstorming

The IB provides a wealth of guidance online and in the extended essay support material. If you do not already have access to the subject-specific guidance for the extended essay, ask your coordinator or supervisor to share it with you. Start with the courses you enjoy or excel in, and review the subject-specific guidance for those areas. This will provide you with sample topics, and by exploring the material, you will be reminded of the types of questions, issues, and themes the subject addresses.

If you already know that you are interested in one or two subjects, you can use the following activities to begin narrowing in on a subject-specific (or interdisciplinary) topic.

Activity

1. Spend some time reading recent articles related to your subject. For example, you could search online using the subject as a keyword along with a term like 'news' or 'issues'. For example, you might enter 'business management current issues' or 'literature news' or 'advances in mathematics'. Allow time to browse and skim articles and information, making notes in your RRS.
2. Using your school's library, or media resources, or an internet search, browse through recent scholarly papers in your chosen subject. Look for features such as 'future research directions' or 'recommendations for further research' often found at the end of academic journal articles and studies. As you read, note recurring terminology and key words in your RRS, as this can help you find relevant sources once you begin your formal research phase.
3. Consider an idea, fact, theory or material you have seen or learned and pretend that you must take a new approach to it, or apply a new theory, or pose a **counter-argument** on that subject. You could also consider pairing that idea, theory or study with something very different to see if new questions or approaches might arise. For example:
   - Flip the perspective. Instead of considering how algorithms can be designed to drive users to content they would like, consider the creation of an algorithm that would help users discover content they would not normally encounter, to promote content diversity. (Computer Science)
   - Focus on gaps and exceptions. Instead of studying effective designs, explore how seemingly confusing or inefficient designs achieve success. (Design Technology)
   - Consider the unique perspective you might bring. If you study dance, consider how dance

principles might be applied to other fields or to problems in those fields, such as using dance principles to understand kinaesthetic learning. (Dance and Psychology – Interdisciplinary pathway)
- Consider applying the approaches and theories from one field of study to another subject: explore the quantum physics of multiple timelines in fantasy literature. (Physics and Language A)

4. Take a topic of interest to you and approach it from multiple angles. For example, you might consider the study of anaerobic training (Sports, Exercise and Health Science), and write about it in your RRS from the following angles:
   - Describe and define it (anaerobic training).
   - Compare it to a similar topic in SEHS and then to a very different topic, noting the ways in which the topic is described, approached and tested in similar and different ways.
   - Associate it – what is this topic related to? What does it impact and what influences it?
   - Dissect it – take it apart and explain its components and the factors involved.
   - Argue in favour of it and then against it.

As you write, take note of any patterns, recurring ideas or questions that emerge.

Now you try it

Choose one or more of the activities above to help you begin thinking of subject-specific or interdisciplinary topics, recording your ideas in your RRS. You may wish to pause at different moments and do a little background reading as ideas and questions arise, so allow yourself some time to do this without rushing.

Narrowing your topic

It may be a good idea to come up with two or three topics, so that if your first one does not work, you have more ready. Once you have these topics, it is time to narrow your focus. As you work through this process, remember what you learned in Chapter 3 about the characteristics of a good research question. It should be:

- clear
- focused
- analytical
- realistic
- measurable
- relevant.

Activity

Ask yourself a series of 'limiting' questions to refine your subject into a general topic, which you will then narrow, bit by bit. For example:

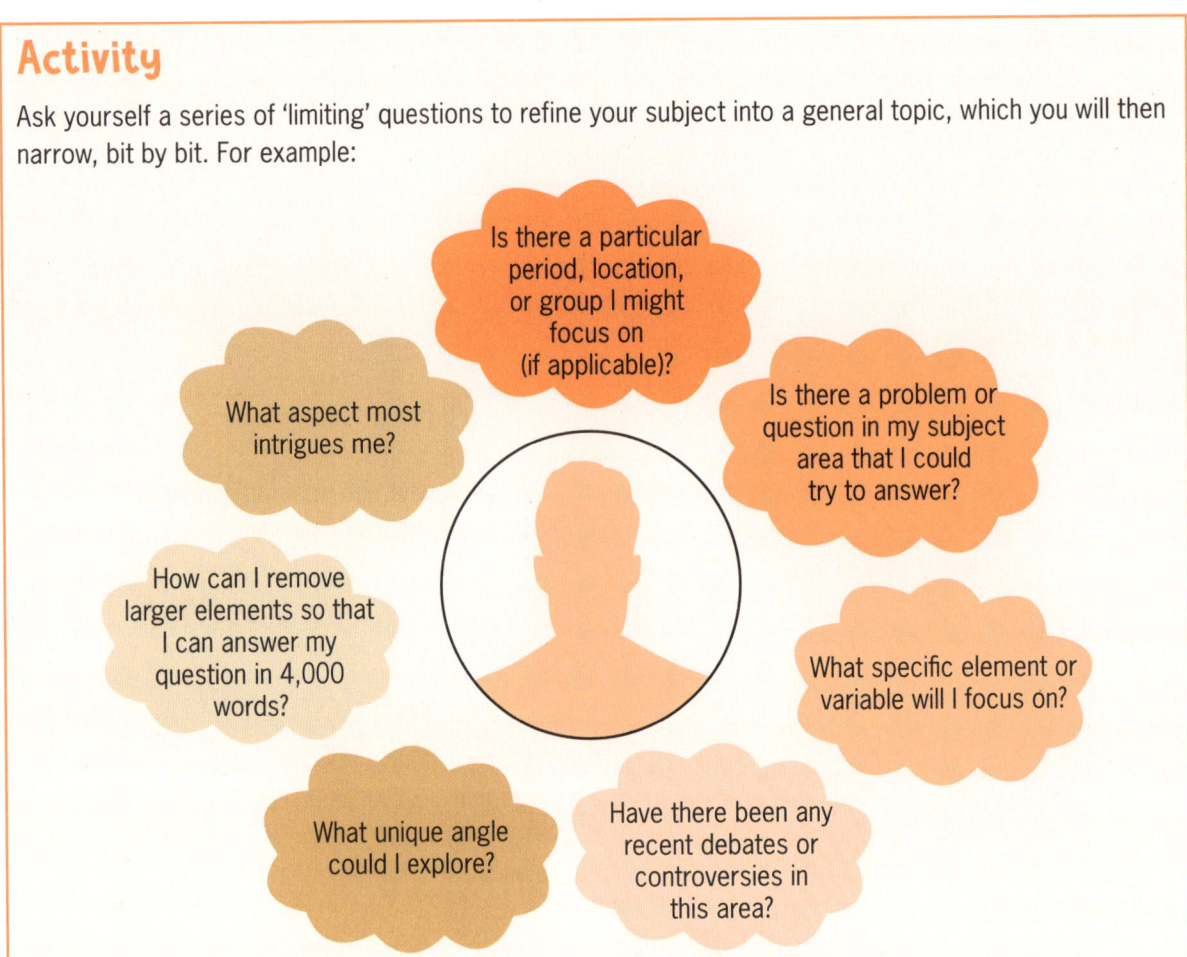

Now you try it

Start with your general subject or subjects of interest and write them at the top of a piece of paper or document in your RRS. Then ask yourself the series of questions above to refine your subject into one that is appropriate for the extended essay. Allow yourself time for background reading if needed.

Example

Mathilde's subject: Social and Cultural Anthropology

What aspects of social and cultural anthropology intrigue me?	Cultures, identities and how they are formed
Are there particular parts of these elements of anthropology that I like?	I recently saw a video on hip-hop as a form of cultural identity formation, which made me interested in exploring some sort of music. I already like rap and pop music.

Narrower topic	Music and cultural identity
What aspect or element of music?	Rap or pop
Narrowing further	I've done some general reading online using search terms 'rap' and 'hip-hop' as well as 'anthropology' and 'culture'. I've found that I'm mostly interested in the use of music and storytelling as a form of preserving a culture.
What culture or geographical location could I focus on as a case study for the larger issue?	I've done some more internet browsing and background research. Since I'm Canadian, I've been mostly researching rappers in Montréal and Toronto.
What kind of culture are these rappers preserving?	Caribbean. I've carried out a bit more reading and have focused specifically on Haitian culture in rap from Montréal.
What period?	The past 20 years
Focused research question	'In what ways and to what extent have Montréal rappers preserved Haitian cultural practices through their music since 2000?'

Example

Qian's subject: Physics

What aspects of physics intrigue me?	Mechanics and thermodynamics
Are there particular parts of these elements that I like?	I'm interested in a career in renewable energy that involves the use of physics, so I did some background reading and found some videos related to construction materials for energy-efficient homes. I'm intrigued by the decisions facing engineers regarding building materials for energy absorption and retention.
Narrower topic	Something to do with different building materials and how they absorb and retain solar energy. I then did more brainstorming and background reading to narrow my focus and identify a definite topic.
Focused research question	'To what extent do the physical properties of building materials (specifically thickness and pigmentation) influence their thermal absorption and heat retention capacities, and what are the implications for sustainable architectural design?'

Example

Gerry's subject: Visual Arts

What aspects of visual arts do I like?	Movements like surrealism, pop art, abstract art
What about those movements intrigues me?	Through some mind-mapping, I realised that I am fascinated by art that tries to reach people on a subconscious level; art that does not use recognisable images to get at deeper emotional truths; art that challenges beliefs and is very personal.
Narrowing in on a topic	I did some background reading and research on these topics using key words such as 'visual art' and 'subconscious', and 'abstract' and 'emotions'. I found that there is a lot of scholarship on the overlap between philosophy and postmodern pop art. So, I read some more on those specific topics and decided that the interdisciplinary pathway might offer an interesting approach to the topic, using the concepts and approaches of IB Philosophy and Visual Arts.
Narrower topic	Postmodern philosophy and pop art
Which artists or types of art could I use as my case study? And which aspect of postmodern philosophy could I use in connection?	After some more reading and some discussion with my IB Philosophy teacher, I decided to look at artists who critiqued beliefs about what constitutes fine art (that is, art that belongs in a museum or is considered 'high'). I read a lot about how artists like Andy Warhol and Roy Lichtenstein challenged grand narratives about the boundaries between high and low culture, but I want to select a lesser-known artist so that I can offer some original ideas and apply tenets of postmodern philosophy to my analysis of their sculptures.
Focused research question	'To what extent did artist Marisol Escobar use postmodern philosophy to challenge the boundaries between high and low art during the 1960s and 1970s?'

Responsible AI use in your research process

Unlike internet searches that simply retrieve information, **AI tools** can help you brainstorm, refine ideas and make connections between concepts. The key is crafting thoughtful prompts rather than simple queries. For example, instead of typing 'military technology First World War', you might prompt: 'Explain three innovative military technologies from the First World War and their strategic impact, focusing on less-discussed examples.' While AI can synthesise information across sources, it is essential to verify any facts or claims with credible academic sources before incorporating them into your work.

AI outputs should inspire your thinking but never replace proper research verification. Remember that AI can make mistakes, present outdated information or even generate data that sounds plausible but is incorrect.

Use AI-generated ideas only as starting points that lead you toward authoritative sources and deeper exploration. A research question should ultimately reflect your genuine curiosity and understanding and be supported by verified research.

Chapter 6 offers more guidance on using AI tools in your research, while Chapter 8 outlines the IB's policies and procedures for using and properly citing these tools.

Deciding on a pathway

As you explore topics and devise a working research question, keep an open mind about which pathway you will choose: subject-focused or interdisciplinary (see Chapter 1). For many topics, either pathway could work – it just depends on the focus you end up taking.

For example, you may be interested in a geography topic that also seems to involve some history. Certainly, within your IB Geography course you will explore historical facts, elements and studies as you learn about the subject. However, as you look into extended essay topics on the subject of geography, you may find that your focus is a current question such as population distribution based on food availability, or you may realise that your geography question could be more richly developed by exploring it through a historical lens, in which case the interdisciplinary pathway might be a better fit.

> ### Remember
> The IB provides a wealth of possible topics, both subject-specific and interdisciplinary, within the extended essay guide and other support materials, so be sure to access and use those resources to supplement the information here.

Frameworks for the interdisciplinary pathway

The IB has defined five 'frameworks' to help you think about your interdisciplinary topic in a meaningful way. Like many of the key concepts and lenses with which you approach your studies in Diploma Programme coursework (such as key concepts in History or Areas of Exploration in Literature), these frameworks can help you think critically about the larger ideas and issues that your topic seeks to address, even if it does not do so explicitly in the essay. The categories are broad and flexible, with a great deal of overlap and interconnection. As you begin exploring interdisciplinary possibilities, consider the five frameworks and try to determine which one(s) your topic connects to. You should identify the framework explicitly on the title page of your extended essay (see Chapter 11).

Interdisciplinary extended essay frameworks

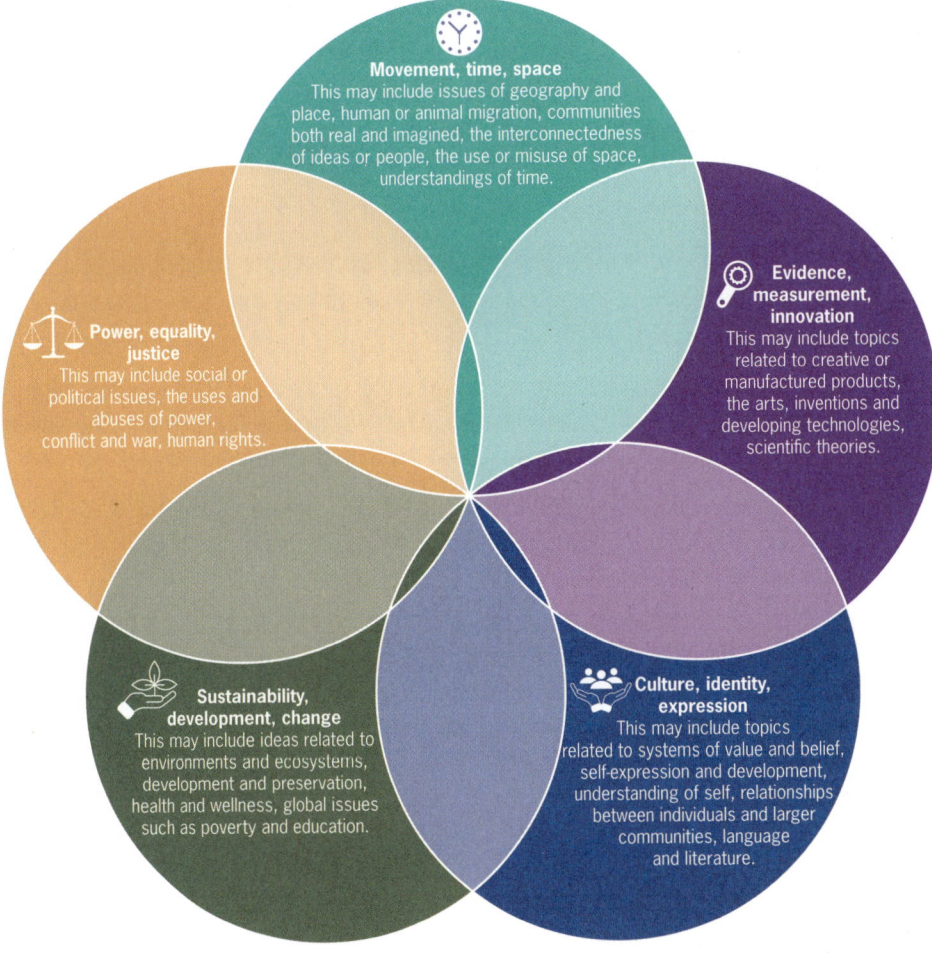

> ### Remember
> Each of these frameworks is discussed in more detail in the extended essay material provided by IB, which your supervisor or coordinator can provide.

Although an interdisciplinary extended essay must be registered in one of these five frameworks, you decide how to define the framework and apply it in a way that works well for you. Your extended essay will not be directly assessed according to your chosen framework – the framework is intended to help you conceptualise your topic in a meaningful way.

You might also consider entering one or more of these frameworks into an AI tool or search engine, along with key words related to your interest and two IB Diploma Programme subjects, to see if these tools can provide inspiration for integrating the two subjects using concepts from the framework. Look at the following example.

> ### Example
> **AI prompt:** 'Offer some ideas for research topics combining IB Global Politics and Philosophy, using the broad conceptual framework of power, equality and justice.'

Results from AI tool:

(Anthropic. (2024). Claude [Large Language Model].)

Global justice and climate change ethics

Examine how philosophical theories of justice can inform international climate policy, particularly exploring:

- the moral obligations of low-income countries versus high-income countries
- intergenerational justice in climate action
- the philosophical basis for climate reparations
- theories of collective responsibility applied to environmental harm.

Digital power and democratic theory

Analyse how modern technology affects traditional concepts of political power:

- social media's impact on democratic deliberation and public discourse
- digital sovereignty in an interconnected world
- the philosophical implications of algorithmic governance
- the tension between privacy rights and digital surveillance.

Global economic inequality and theories of justice

Investigate how different philosophical frameworks approach global wealth disparities:

- Rawlsian theories of justice applied to international economic systems
- the moral foundations of global redistributive policies
- philosophy of borders and economic migration rights
- competing conceptions of economic fairness across cultures.

Sovereignty and human rights

Explore the philosophical tension between state sovereignty and universal human rights:

- the philosophical justification for humanitarian intervention
- cultural relativism versus universal human rights
- the evolution of sovereignty in a globalised world
- 'Collective versus individual rights in international law'.

You can then use any of these to begin your own research and background reading. However, make sure that the topic you pursue falls clearly into two IB Diploma Programme subjects and is feasible using the methods, approaches and content of the courses themselves, as AI will not always offer IB- or extended essay-specific ideas.

Now you try it

Now that you have explored various methods for narrowing your topic and understand the characteristics of strong research questions from Chapter 3, you are ready to develop working research questions for your own extended essay topic. Draft at least three possible research questions for your own extended essay topic. Evaluate each one using the criteria for strong research questions (clear, focused, analytical, realistic, measurable and relevant). Select the strongest one and explain why you believe it meets all six criteria. If you are still not satisfied with any of your questions, what specific improvements do you need to make?

| Your extended essay topic | |

Research questions	Evaluation (✓ for yes)		
1.	☐ Clear ☐ Realistic	☐ Focused ☐ Measurable	☐ Analytical ☐ Relevant
2.	☐ Clear ☐ Realistic	☐ Focused ☐ Measurable	☐ Analytical ☐ Relevant
3.	☐ Clear ☐ Realistic	☐ Focused ☐ Measurable	☐ Analytical ☐ Relevant

| Strongest question | |

Improvements needed:

Key takeaways: Chapter 4

- Choose a topic that genuinely interests you and can sustain your attention over months of research, while also making sure it allows for analysis and argument rather than just fact-finding. The topic should align with at least one IB Diploma subject that you are studying.
- Use brainstorming techniques to develop your topic, including general questioning (about your interests and future goals), subject-specific research (reading recent articles and scholarly papers), and mind-mapping. You can also use AI tools for initial brainstorming, although the final research question must be your own.
- Narrow down your topic systematically by asking limiting questions about specific aspects, time periods, locations or **variables** you want to focus on. Engage in background reading throughout this phase, as this will also help you narrow and refine your topic. The goal is to develop a research question that is clear, focused, analytical, realistic, measurable and relevant enough to be addressed within 4,000 words.

Key terms

AI tools: software that uses artificial intelligence algorithms to solve problems and perform tasks

counter-argument: a set of reasons set forward to oppose or disprove an idea that has been developed in another argument

data: a collection or series of facts, observations or measurements, often presented in the form of numbers or letters

mind map: a diagram that visually represents ideas, using a central idea, with associated ideas ranged around it, connected by lines

perspective: a particular way of thinking about something, especially one that is influenced by someone's own beliefs or experiences

variable: a factor that can change in quantity, quality or size, which must be taken into consideration in a situation

Chapter 5 – Understanding your selected IB subject(s)

This chapter covers the following:
- Knowing and understanding your subject
- Command terms and the extended essay
- Subject-specific overviews
- Combining subjects in an Interdisciplinary extended essay

Learner profile traits
Open-minded
Knowledgeable
Thinkers

Knowing and understanding your subject

Regardless of which pathway you end up selecting, your success will rely largely on your knowledge and understanding of theories, frameworks, concepts and methods of your chosen subject(s). As you research and write in your chosen subject(s), stop at regular intervals and think *about* what you are reading, thinking and writing. This is called **metacognition** and is the main aim of your theory of knowledge course.

Activity

To guide your metacognitive thinking, ask questions such as:

Now you try it

In your RRS, try to answer most or all the questions above for the subject(s) you are thinking of pursuing for your extended essay. If you have trouble answering them, speak with your subject teacher or another expert, or do some research on your subject – its history, approaches and methods, theories, its ways of producing knowledge, and so on. If you can explain the nature and purpose of your subject, your essay will be more accurate, informed and effective.

Command terms and the extended essay

As you encountered in Chapter 3, command terms are usually **action verbs** that identify specific tasks – words such as 'evaluate', 'assess', 'examine' and 'compare'. While these terms can shape effective research questions, they also serve a much broader purpose throughout the extended essay process.

Command terms function as a specialised language that connects your understanding of subject-specific methodologies with the formal assessment requirements. They reflect the disciplinary thinking patterns valued within each subject and signal the depth of critical engagement expected in academic discourse.

Command terms are important because ...

1. They shape your research approach and methodology. Different command terms require different types of evidence and analysis. For example, 'evaluate' requires you to consider both strengths and weaknesses, while 'analyse' focuses on breaking down components.

2. They determine the depth and type of critical thinking required.
   - 'Compare' involves examining similarities and differences.
   - 'Justify' requires you to prove your position with evidence.
   - 'Discuss' needs a balanced exploration of different perspectives.

3. They help focus your research question.
   - The command term you choose helps define the scope of your investigation.
   - It determines the kind of sources and evidence you will need.
   - It helps you stay focused during research and writing.

4. They align with the extended essay assessment criteria.
   - Criterion A assesses your choice, explanation and use of appropriate research methods as the framework for approaching your topic.
   - Criterion C evaluates your ability to analyse effectively, evaluate your findings and maintain a focused line of argument.
   - Criterion D measures your discussion and evaluation of your findings using relevant evidence.

In Chapter 3, you explored command terms for research questions. They also reflect how disciplines approach knowledge. For example, History often uses 'to what extent' questions, showing its concern with nuance and multiple factors. Sciences favour 'analyse' and 'investigate', reflecting **empirical** approaches. Literature tends toward 'examine' and 'explore', indicating interpretive methods.

These terms also align with assessment criteria: 'evaluate' connects to Criterion D (Discussion and evaluation), while 'analyse' relates to Criterion C (Analysis and line of argument).

Understanding the command terms of your subject demonstrates your grasp of its methodological conventions and helps structure your thinking.

Subject-specific overviews

You must be able to define and explain what constitutes knowledge and evidence in your chosen subject(s), as well as how research and data collection are done in these areas. In addition to reviewing the materials and knowledge from the Diploma Programme course itself, read the subject-specific extended essay guidance for each subject you are interested in.

Below you will find brief overviews of each of the six IB **subject groups**. Note that within these groups there are often several individual subjects, each with its own distinct requirements, expectations and considerations. This is why it is important to know and understand your subject(s)!

> ### Remember
> Remember that the extended essay is a self-directed process, so that it is ultimately *your* responsibility, not your supervisor's, to know and understand the requirements of an extended essay in that subject(s). This is especially true if you choose an interdisciplinary pathway, as your supervisor may not be familiar with the requirements of a subject they do not teach.

Language A

An extended essay in Language A (the primary language in which you are completing the IB Diploma):

- engages in literary and/or rhetorical criticism by analysing one or more texts
- discusses the author or authors' structural and stylistic choices (including literary and/or rhetorical devices and techniques) and the meaning they create
- uses existing scholarship and/or critical theory to shape and inform the analysis.

Requirements and specifications

- A Language A extended essay must focus on at least one text or work originally written in that language. Significant point penalties are applied across several grading criteria if you write an essay solely on a translated work.
- It can explore a single text in depth or perform a comparative analysis of more than one work.
- It can focus on either literature or a language text.
- It may pair the work with a work or works read in translation for a comparative study.
- The focus of the essay should be on the literary or language text and not a social, philosophical or political issue. This means that you may discuss a real-life issue (for example, the search for

identity) but your discussion must remain grounded in the text, and should analyse how that real-life issue is portrayed in the work using various literary, rhetorical, structural and stylistic techniques.
- Choose texts that offer sufficient depth and complexity to sustain thorough literary analysis. Works with an established body of criticism can provide valuable secondary sources to support your investigation. You might consider pairing a less **canonical** text with a more traditionally 'literary' work.
- If your text is a film, you must discuss the screenplay just as you would the script of a play, and include consideration of visual, auditory and other non-verbal elements.
- Your essay must make use of both primary (your work under exploration) and secondary (literary criticism and scholarly research) sources.
- You may not use a work that you have studied in your Language A course, although you may select a different work by the same author.
- If you choose to compare two works, you should make clear why pairing these works for analysis enriches understanding and appreciation of them both.

Sample topics for Language A (Using English as the Language A)

- 'How do Audre Lorde's poetry collection *The Black Unicorn* (1978) and Bhanu Kapil's *The Vertical Interrogation of Strangers* (2001) explore the role of hair as a symbol of cultural identity and assimilation in immigrant and diasporic narratives?'
- 'How has TikTok's algorithmic promotion of AAVE (African American Vernacular English) influenced its adoption and transformation among non-Black Gen Z users from 2020 to 2024?'
- 'How do Patrick Süskind's *Perfume* (1985) and George Orwell's *Animal Farm* (1945) use the manipulation of sensory experience as a metaphor for political control?'

Language B

An extended essay in Language B:

- offers an opportunity to strengthen and enrich your fluency in, and knowledge of, the second language you are studying in your IB Diploma Programme and the culture(s) associated with that language
- can focus on either a literary work in that language, an aspect of the culture, the use of the language itself, or a combination of these.

Requirements and specifications

- The text or texts being studied must have originally been written in Language B.
- If you choose the screenplay of a film, you should focus on the language rather than any cinematographic techniques or elements.
- If you choose to analyse texts, be sure to select ones (even non-traditional texts) that have a range of secondary sources associated with them.
- Your essay must make use of both primary (your works under exploration) and secondary (literary/cultural criticism and scholarly research) sources.
- If you are going to study a culture associated with the language, you must:
  ○ focus on a social or cultural issue that is unique to the language
  ○ explore the topic as it influences the use or form of the language *or* explore the topic using some form of cultural evidence (or 'artefact') such as a concrete object like a literary or creative work.

- In addition to your primary source(s), most of your secondary sources (if not all) should also be written in the target language.

Sample topics

- (Translated from Language B: Spanish into the language of this textbook): 'How has the rise of voice-activated assistants like Alexa and Siri influenced the adaptation of Spanish command forms and politeness markers in Mexico?'
- (Translated from Language B: German into the language of this textbook): 'How does Patrick Süskind's *Das Parfum* use the motif of scent and olfactory imagery to represent the protagonist's isolation from and manipulation of society?'
- (For an IB Diploma Candidate for whom Language B is English): 'How did Barack Obama's use of anaphora and parallel structure in his major speeches from 2004 to 2008 reflect and reinforce themes of national unity?'

Individuals and Societies (including Business Management, Economics, Digital Society, Geography, Global Politics, History, Philosophy, Psychology, Social and Cultural Anthropology, and World Religions)

An extended essay in an Individuals and Societies subject:

- offers you the chance to explore a topic related to human experience
- provides a multitude of perspectives and frameworks through which to select a topic
- can explore a topic of current global interest or an issue from another time or place.

Requirements and specifications

- Most Individuals and Societies extended essays require a combination of primary and secondary sources *except* Psychology and Social and Cultural Anthropology:
  - An extended essay in Social and Cultural Anthropology will need to rely primarily on existing ethnographic studies and on secondary sources (unlike your IA, which is based primarily on your own fieldwork and other primary sources).
  - An extended essay in Psychology must be based on secondary sources (such as existing studies) only (unlike your IA in Psychology, which requires you to replicate an existing study and gather your own primary data).
- Because there are so many subjects within the Individuals and Societies category, it is important that you know and understand the specifics of your selected subject, including the guidelines on what constitutes appropriate primary and secondary sources, data, evidence and theories.
- Carefully read any subject-specific guidance and the course syllabus on your selected subject (or subjects, in an Interdisciplinary essay). If you are unsure, ask a teacher in that subject or your supervisor. Remember – this is your project and the ultimate responsibility for accuracy falls on you.

Sample topics

- 'To what extent have IoT-enabled smart classrooms enhanced elementary student mathematics learning outcomes in the United States?' (Digital Society)
- 'To what extent did the 2022 Nord Stream pipeline explosions transform energy security cooperation and diplomatic relations between Germany and Russia?' (Global Politics)
- 'To what extent does the rise of algorithmic decision-making in financial markets challenge traditional concepts of moral responsibility and market rationality?' (Interdisciplinary, combining Philosophy and Economics)

The Sciences (Including Biology, Chemistry, Computer Science, Design Technology, Physics, and Sports, Exercise and Health Science)

An extended essay in a Sciences subject:

- investigates a scientific research question by gathering primary or secondary data through experimentation
- must make a valid conclusion based on sound evidence
- relies on scientific method.

Requirements and specifications

- Your science extended essay can take a variety of approaches. It can be:
  - based on **raw data** (either your own or the raw or processed data of another scientist, which you analyse)
  - based on an experiment that you design and perform
  - undertaken using a theoretical approach, in which you create, test and analyse a model
  - a **quantitative** or **qualitative analysis** of a larger phenomenon, using a **survey**
  - a combination of any of the above.
- If you are conducting an experiment, it should be feasible for you to complete it in time and using the resources available to you.
- An experiment should be conducted under the supervision of a teacher at your school.
- It should use the International System of Units (SI).
- Do not be concerned if the results of your experiment do not prove your hypothesis! Both negative and positive results are useful in your discussion and evaluation.
- If you are conducting an experiment that involves human subjects (such as in Sports, Exercise and Health Sciences), you must follow all guidelines and regulations set out by the IB regarding informed consent, ethical considerations and confidentiality requirements. Remember that you are not permitted to perform any experiment on humans or animals that might cause anxiety, pain or any risk for the participants. A full explanation of these guidelines can be found on the IBO website.

Sample topics

- (Biology) 'How does exposure to common household plant pathogens affect the growth and defense response of garden tomatoes (*Solanum lycopersicum*), as measured by visible symptoms and plant growth parameters?'
- (Sports, Exercise and Health Science) 'How accurate are wrist-worn fitness trackers in measuring heart rate compared to traditional chest strap monitors during different types of exercise intensities?'
- (Design Technology) 'To what extent has the transition from aluminium to carbon-fibre frames affected racing bicycle performance metrics in professional road cycling from 2010 to 2024?'

Mathematics

An extended essay in Mathematics:

- can be theoretical (focusing on 'pure' mathematical concepts, proofs and abstract thinking) or practical (applying mathematical concepts to real-world questions or problems), or a combination of both
- offers you the opportunity to apply mathematics to a topic of interest to you
- may be shorter than 4,000 words because of the amount of algebra included in your essay.

Requirements and specifications

- For more theoretical essays, your research will involve reading and selecting key secondary sources related to the theory.
- Ensure you are comfortable with the mathematics theory or concept you will be using and demonstrate that understanding in your introduction.
- For practical essays, your approach should be driven by the data, but it should also be flexible: avoid specifying the mathematical or statistical methods you will be using in your research question. You may only determine the best analytical techniques after you have examined your data thoroughly. Your research might, therefore, involve learning and explaining mathematical concepts that were not in your original plan, but became necessary based on what your data revealed.
- The strength of your essay lies in how effectively you apply mathematical concepts to analyse your data and address your research question, not necessarily in the complexity of the mathematics used.
- Use raw data that you will then analyse, rather than data that has already been processed by someone else (for example, rather than working with published unemployment rates, you should gather your own data).

Sample topics

- 'How do variations in the complex quadratic polynomial $z^2 + c$ affect the boundary properties of the Mandelbrot set, and what mathematical patterns emerge from these variations?'
- 'How effectively can statistical methods identify and quantify the relationship between daily temperature fluctuations and local electricity consumption?'
- 'Using location optimisation theory, what is the most efficient distribution of emergency response units in Toulouse, France to minimise average response time based on historical emergency call data?'

The Arts (Including Dance, Theatre, Visual Arts, Film and Music)

An extended essay in an Arts subject:

- can investigate a wide range of creative products and practices
- explores how the arts reflect human experience
- should be based on an analysis of primary sources (the works of art themselves) as well as secondary, scholarly resources.

Requirements and specifications

- If you are writing on visual art, dance or music, your essay should include sufficient primary sources to sustain meaningful and thorough analysis (for example, more than one sculpture or painting).
- Ensure you are comfortable with the methods of analysis of your selected subject, as well as the appropriate terminology.
- Make sure that your topic is focused on the artistic creation itself. This means that you may discuss a real-life issue such as a theme (for example, the loss of innocence) or a socio-political issue explored by the works, but your primary concern is to explore how the artist conveys this idea using the creative techniques available to them. Avoid topics that:
  - focus primarily on the artist's biography
  - attempt to prove one artist's influence on another
  - are more historical review of an artistic movement or artist than a close reading of art pieces
  - focus on song lyrics or the social/historical evolution of a type of music – instead, analyse the music *as* music – discussing structure, style and technical elements.

Sample topics

- (Dance) 'How have African dance elements been integrated and transformed in Alvin Ailey's major works, particularly in *Revelations* (1960) and *Cry* (1971)?'
- (Theatre) 'How did Bertolt Brecht's alienation effect revolutionise audience engagement in political theatre, as demonstrated in *Mother Courage and Her Children* and *The Caucasian Chalk Circle?*'
- (Film) 'How did Satyajit Ray's use of naturalistic lighting and on-location shooting in *Pather Panchali* (1955) challenge the studio-bound conventions of 1950s Indian cinema?'

Cross-disciplinary subjects (Including Environmental Systems and Societies, and Literature and Performance)

Although Environmental Systems and Societies and Literature and Performance each **integrate** more than one discipline, these subjects are classified by the IB as 'cross-disciplinary' and single subject-focused. Because they are already interdisciplinary by nature, it is best not to combine either of them with a separate subject. That would probably create a more complicated topic than can be reasonably addressed in 4,000 words!

Requirements and specifications

An Environmental Systems and Societies extended essay offers the opportunity to explore an environmental topic by examining it through the methods and theories of the humanities, such as economics, geography and other fields of human society.

There are many possible topics for an essay on ESS, but whatever you choose, make sure that the focus is on the interaction between humans and the natural environment.

Sample topics

- 'How do household income and ethnicity influence participation rates in recycling programmes across different Singapore neighbourhoods, particularly examining the effectiveness of blue bin initiatives?'
- 'To what extent is Brazil's soybean industry in the Mato Grosso region threatened by extreme weather events and shifting rainfall patterns driven by Amazon deforestation?'

A Literature and Performance extended essay must focus on both a written text (such as a novel or play) and a performance (such as a film, theatre staging or digital adaptation) of that piece.

Combining subjects in an Interdisciplinary extended essay

Choosing the interdisciplinary pathway means you feel that your research question can best be answered using elements from two subjects. However, there is no single 'right' way to do this – there are countless ways to integrate two subjects.

> ### Activity
>
> You could compile a list of the frameworks, concepts, approaches and knowledge-making practices of each subject, using the responses to the questions you answered on page 43. You might consider creating a **Venn diagram**, which allows you to note ways in which the two subjects overlap. Then, think about your topic with that diagram in mind. Which elements of each subject might be best to use in investigating your topic? Is there some overlap (shared methodologies, theories or areas of inquiry) which might offer a natural way to combine the subjects?

Example

Sean enjoys reading and interpreting literature but has been intrigued by activities in his Language A: Literature class in which students were asked to quantify and track particular literary and poetic devices. He wondered how he might use what he has learned in Computer Science to complete that kind of work, which then led him to wonder about the limitations of both subjects in arriving at literary interpretation. He made a Venn diagram of the methods, theories and concepts of both courses.

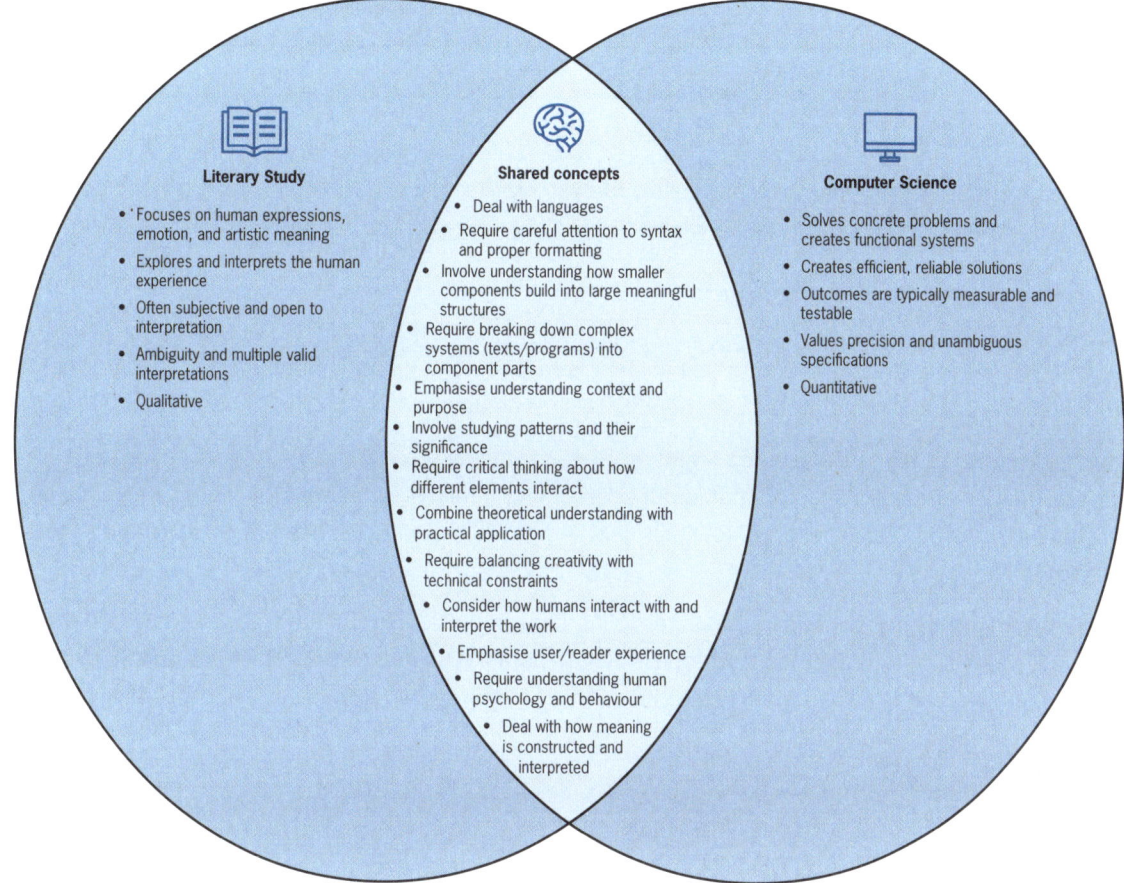

Sean noticed that the middle portion of the diagram showed how both disciplines look for patterns and then try to generate meaning from those patterns. Both can use systematic observation to organise information, and both subjects rely to some extent on logic and reasoning to make valid interpretations of data. Where they differ is in their approach to ambiguity, since the sciences tend to eliminate ambiguity while literature often embraces it.

Subjects: Computer Science and Literature

Research question: 'To what extent do Natural Language Processing algorithms interpret and analyse metaphors in contemporary poetry, such as that of Ocean Vuong, better than traditional literary analysis methods?'

For this extended essay, the student wanted to see how something subjective like poetry might be analysed in a more objective, mathematical way. He decided to compare his understanding and analysis of Ocean Vuong's poetry to the pattern recognition, structural analysis, and algorithms of his Computer Science course. This approach led to insights such as:

- how algorithms might miss layers of meaning that human readers catch
- why some types of metaphors are harder to detect computationally
- how machine learning could enhance (but not replace) literary analysis
- where human interpretation and computational analysis complement each other
- what computational analysis reveals about patterns in metaphor construction that humans might miss.

Now you try it

Using the previous activity and example, follow the same process in your RRS for both of your selected subjects. Create a Venn diagram to see where the subjects overlap and see what insights that leads you to.

If you feel that you might focus more on one subject, see if you can identify some gaps in the information, approach or ways of knowing that the other subject might be able to fill.

As you begin to write, try to show how insights from each subject strengthen your overall analysis or discussion. Use concepts from both fields to analyse your findings and see if that yields new understandings. In your essay, explain how that new understanding was achieved by the pairing of these two subjects.

Remember to remain open-minded in these beginning phases of the extended essay. You may find that what you thought was a single subject-focused topic might benefit from an interdisciplinary approach. On the other hand, a topic you felt was naturally interdisciplinary might end up being easily addressed in a single subject. Both situations are okay!

Key takeaways: Chapter 5

- Knowledge and understanding of your chosen subject(s) are critical for success in the IB extended essay.
- Most subjects have specific requirements and considerations. These can be found in the subject-specific guidance section of the IB extended essay guide.
- Interdisciplinary essays need clear and purposeful integration of the two subjects.
- It is helpful to remain open-minded and flexible in your beginning phases as you brainstorm, identify subject areas and narrow topics.

Key terms

action verbs: verbs that describe the action that the subject of a sentence performs

canonical: describing something that belongs to an officially recognised group of writings

empirical: based on observation and experience rather than on theory

ethical: relating to rules or conduct and beliefs about what is morally right or wrong

integrate: to meaningfully combine and synthesise concepts, methodologies and insights from two subjects

metacognition: the process of thinking about one's own mental processes

moral: relating to personal beliefs about what is right or wrong

qualitative analysis: an analysis based on non-quantifiable data, such as experiences or behaviour

quantitative analysis: an analysis that uses maths and statistics, considering different sizes and amounts

raw data: data that has not been processed, changed or analysed in any way (also known as primary data)

subject group: one of the six IB Diploma Programme subject categories, Language A (Group 1), Language B (Group 2), Individuals and Societies (Group 3), Sciences (Group 4), Mathematics (Group 5) and The Arts (Group 6)

survey: a way of gathering information by asking people a series of specific questions

Venn diagram: a diagram that uses overlapping circles to show the separate and shared features of two or more sets of information

Chapter 6 – Research methods and strategies

> **This chapter covers the following:**
> - The research phase
> - Types of sources
> - Finding and evaluating sources
> - Using sources
> - Using AI tools in research
> - Organising your research materials

> **Learner profile traits**
> Knowledgeable
> Thinkers
> Reflective

The research phase

Once you have your working research question and feel comfortable with your subject(s), you will dive more deeply into focused research so that you can:

- gather knowledge about your topic and subject(s)
- critically read and assess existing thought and scholarship on your topic and within your subject(s)
- use the above to begin shaping your thought and argument
- journey towards a thesis statement, which will be the response to your research question.

As with other parts of the extended essay process, your research phase will be recursive – that is, your research will be a process of thinking, reading, rethinking, perhaps changing focus or following new leads, or returning at times to earlier thinking.

Activity

You began doing research as you explored topics and crafted your research question (see Chapter 4). If you kept detailed, organised research notes during your background reading, you may wish to return to those and remind yourself of the sources you identified as particularly helpful or as worthy of reading in full once you began your in-depth research.

Now you try it

Take another look at the sources you consulted during your brainstorming and background reading. Also take a look at your own notes and reflections on those sources, such as questions that arose or points of interest. Locate the original source and read it more deeply and fully this time. Make notes in your RRS to keep track of anything you learn from this that may help you find a 'way in' to this deeper research, especially if you are struggling to begin.

> **Remember**
>
> The research phase of the extended essay is where you become more knowledgeable – and you do this by flexing those thinker muscles. This portion of the extended essay process calls on your use of **conceptual understanding** and exploring knowledge across a range of sources. As you read, you must use critical and creative-thinking skills to analyse and evaluate what you are reading. And as you continue to manage this long-term, self-directed project, you must take responsibility for staying on track.

Types of sources

Think of your extended essay as a scholarly skyscraper. To build something that is both impressive and structurally sound, you need both raw materials (primary sources) and architectural expertise (secondary sources). Primary research involves collecting new information yourself through methods like interviews, experiments or observations. Secondary research means analysing information that others have already gathered and published, such as scholarly articles, books, or reports.

Primary sources: Your raw materials

Primary sources are the fundamental building blocks of your research, and they provide the essential material you will analyse in your investigation. Depending on your subject, they might include the following.

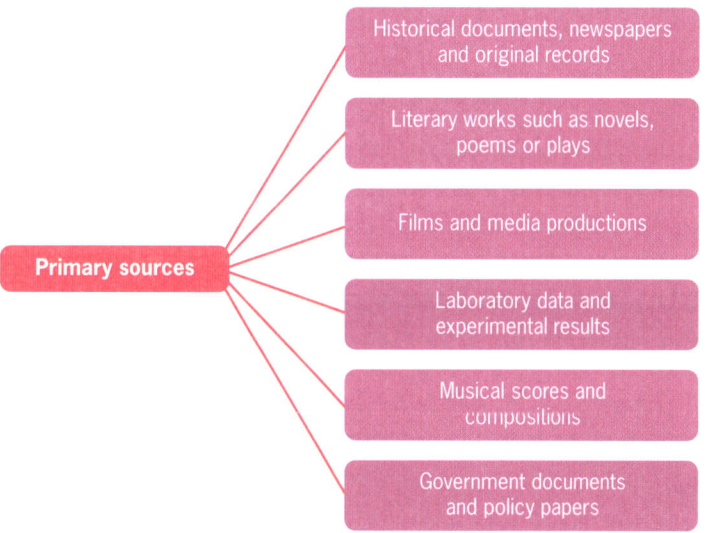

Secondary sources: Your expert blueprint

Like architects consulting established design principles, you will need to understand how other scholars have approached similar work. You can do this by consulting some of the following secondary sources.

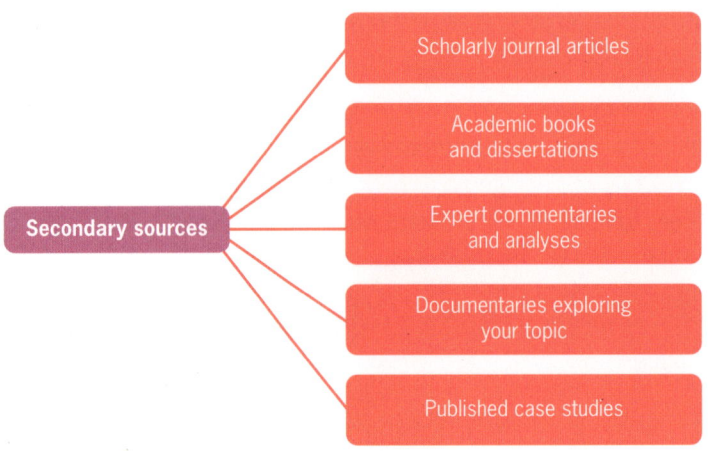

> **Remember**
>
> Be aware that different subjects have different requirements for source types. Most extended essays need both primary and secondary sources, but there are exceptions. For Psychology essays, you should only use secondary sources – collecting your own data is not permitted. For Social and Cultural Anthropology, you will mainly use existing ethnographic materials rather than conducting your own fieldwork. If you are writing in the sciences, you will be generating your own primary data through experiments or investigations.

Finding and evaluating sources

Just as a building needs the right ratio of materials to design principles, your essay needs to balance primary sources, secondary research and your own analysis. This balance is crucial, as Assessment Criteria A, B and D all evaluate how well you integrate these elements within your extended essay. You will explore how to effectively combine these components in Chapter 9, but for now, focus on gathering quality materials and expertise for your academic construction project.

Finding sources

As you have seen, your primary sources will be the documents or literature you plan to analyse or the data you gather when you conduct your own experiment or investigation. Secondary sources may require a bit of creative thinking, flexibility and persistence to locate. Here are a few ideas to get you started.

- Ask your supervisor or Diploma Programme subject teacher to recommend authors, sources, databases, and so on, based on your research question.
- Talk to your school's media specialist or librarian. Librarians are trained research professionals and are invaluable sources of knowledge. They can also help you identify the best search terms, access specialised databases or collections, and connect you with other libraries and research institutions if needed.
- As you continue to consult the sources you found during your background reading, note words, phrases and ideas that you see often. These signal key concepts, terms and issues in the subject that you can use in your own searches.
- Make a list of key concepts in this subject that relate to your research question, even indirectly. If you are enrolled in the course in your Diploma Programme, review your notes and course materials for subject-specific language and ideas.

- Browse books and academic journals on the subject in the media centre or library. Use the table of contents and **index** of books to find the parts that relate to your research question. For example, if you are writing a History essay on military technology in the First World War and pick up a book on the war, skim through the index for the precise locations of terms such as artillery, weapons, innovation, advancement, technology, chemical, aircraft, naval, radio, communication, infantry, and so on. Then look at those pages and determine if any of the information could be useful to you.
- Search research databases available to your school or institution. These databases usually have 'advanced' search engines which can help you quickly limit your searches to a type of article, a date range or to search by author.

Activity

Make a list of concepts, terms, words, phrases and names that:

- come to mind when you think of your subject(s) in general
- come to mind regarding your research question specifically
- you see frequently as you are reading or skimming sources (concepts, theories, methods, subject-specific terminology, and so on)
- keep coming up, such as the name of a scholar or expert who is often quoted or cited.

Example

Amira is writing a Business Management essay on this research question: 'To what extent did the implementation of remote work policies affect employee productivity and organisational culture at tech companies in Singapore between 2020 and 2024?'

Key concepts and terms she has picked up in this course include motivation, organisational behaviour, human resource management, organisational culture, location, revenue.

She also saw these terms again and again as she did her background reading: operational efficiency, remote work policies, employee productivity, employee output metrics, engagement, new technologies.

Experts and scholars whose names keep coming up include Gianpiero Petriglieri, Prithwiraj Choudhury, Nicholas Bloom, Poon King Wang, Lynda Gratton and David Leong.

Amira uses combinations of these terms in order to find a broad range of sources that might be useful for her research question.

(Later, you will see how Amira could use AI tools to target her searches more effectively, as well as to organise the results.)

Now you try it

In your RRS, make a list of the features (concepts, terms, names, and so on) in the activity above. Open a new search in an online academic database and spend some time searching combinations of these words or phrases. Read **abstracts** of articles, skim through reference lists and see how different search term combinations yield different results. Remember to keep detailed citations of what you find, download or print articles for later use, and make note of URLs and the date you accessed the source.

Evaluating sources

The first impulse for many students beginning their research is the use of an internet search engine such as Google. As you probably discovered during your brainstorming and topic-selection phases, these general internet searches can provide basic knowledge of a topic, generate ideas, uncover important terminology and help you focus your interests. However, when you begin your more formal research phase, they will not usually yield the type of academic resources appropriate for an extended essay.

Internet search engines tend to personalise the results you receive based on factors such as your previous search history, your location and even the time of day. Moreover, many search engines involve algorithms intended to maximise paid advertising, or they may return results based on general popularity. Because of this, the results might not be as helpful as a search in an academic database. Similarly, open-access platforms such as Wikipedia, while often helpful for background search, are not peer-reviewed in the same way as academic journal articles. Facts and data may not be reliable and accurate. What makes Wikipedia helpful for general background reading is what also makes it less desirable for deeper research – its articles are intended to be short and easy to read, providing a general overview.

Your extended essay is designed to take you beyond sources like this – to resources that might challenge or expand your thinking. Academic and scholarly work often questions existing theories and beliefs and must provide reliable and convincing evidence to do so. These are the sources you should consult for your extended essay as you, too, enter the world of sophisticated scholarship!

When evaluating how appropriate a source is (especially one not found via an academic database or library), ask yourself if it meets the same standards as your own essay requires: cited sources, detailed and clear methodology, evaluation of analysis, new knowledge or interpretation being produced, and so on.

Appropriate sources

- ✓ Academic research articles
- ✓ Literature reviews/surveys of current scholarship
- ✓ Books published by academic presses (such as Oxford University Press, Harvard University Press, Kluwer/Springer)
- ✓ Edited collections of scholarly papers
- ✓ Research and technical reports from reputable organisations

Sources for background reading/general knowledge gathering only

- Encyclopaedias
- Older or outdated books or scientific findings
- Sources meant for popular audiences
- Museum websites
- Basic textbooks

Unreliable sources

- ✗ Personal opinion blogs (especially those that do not cite sources)
- ✗ Personal social media posts (probably need fact-checking)
- ✗ Personal websites
- ✗ Wikipedia
- ✗ Sites without clear authors
- ✗ Commercial websites
- ✗ Online forums
- ✗ Marketing or propaganda materials
- ✗ Sources without academic or other professional/expert credentials

Using sources

It can be challenging to read dense, **jargon**-filled academic articles related to your topic, but remember that you can use those scholarly papers and books as examples of the kind of academic writing you should be aspiring to in your extended essay. For example, a secondary source will often feature the same components as your extended essay:

- an introduction with a thesis
- an explanation of methodology, frameworks and theories to be used
- a review of the scholarly literature already written on the topic
- evaluation and integration of other sources into the author's own thinking
- body paragraphs of evidence, analysis and discussion
- a conclusion that reviews what has been discussed, addresses the limitations of the study or questions for further, future research, and leaves the reader with a clear sense of the significance of the author's work
- a list of references or works cited, either in **footnotes** or at the end of the paper.

Indeed, it can be helpful to approach secondary sources by looking for these elements. You can use these sources as models for your own work, but understanding the basic organisation of scholarly essays will help you better understand what you are reading. You should also notice the ways in which scholars weave other sources into their writing, particularly how they incorporate evidence and quotations.

Think of your extended essay as a starter kit for the kinds of research and writing you will do at the university and postgraduate levels.

Note-taking and source management

As you do your research, it is vital to keep detailed notes on each source. There are several reasons for this:

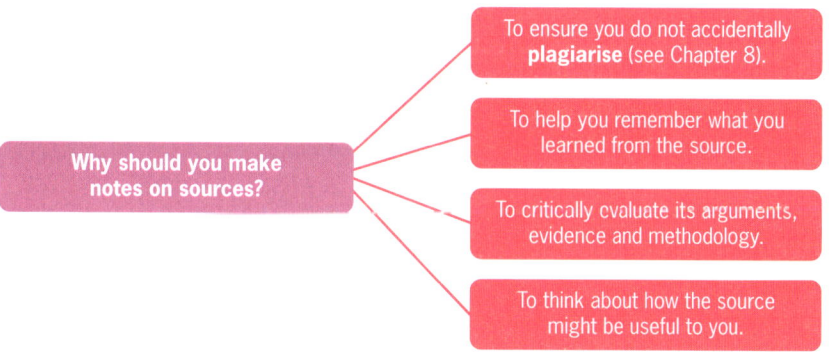

In short, you need to put yourself in active conversation with the source! In doing this, you will also be engaging in reflection. This will help you track your thinking and provide material for your RPF and – by engaging critically with your sources – you transform from a passive reader into a more active scholar, weaving others' insights into your own. Rather than simply echoing others' thoughts, you will learn to **synthesise** various ideas and perspectives.

Activity

It is helpful to create a table to record all the information you need to keep track of. Your table might look something like this:

Source and full citation	Direct quotes	Summary/ paraphrase	Thoughts/ reactions
(Author[s], title, title of larger work or container, publisher, date of publication, page numbers [if applicable], URL or DOI and date you accessed it [if an online source])	(Include page numbers, if applicable)		

You can approach the 'Thoughts/reactions' column in a variety of ways. Below are some ideas to guide you.

Questions to help you think critically about the source itself	Questions to help you identify how the source might help you
<ul><li>What are the author's credentials? How can I tell?</li><li>Why did the author write this article/book/report?</li><li>What kinds of perspectives or biases might shape how this source is presented?</li><li>What are some factors or ideas missing from this source?</li><li>What are some of the source's strengths? Limitations?</li><li>To what extent am I convinced by this source's claims or argument? Why?</li><li>How does this work fit into the larger scholarly conversation? Are there connections to other sources I have read? Is this source building upon or responding to another source?</li></ul>	<ul><li>What is the author's methodology? Is this something I might use, or counter, or rework?</li><li>How is the author proving their argument here? What sort of evidence or data are they using? Do I agree or have a different interpretation? Is there useful information I might synthesise with other information I have?</li><li>Are there gaps or limitations in the source? Might I address those in my investigation?</li><li>To what sources or scholars does this author refer? Might those be useful to me as well?</li><li>In what way might I make use of this source? Does it reinforce my own thinking or might it be used to support my argument? Does it counter or reshape my thinking? Does it offer a different but equally viable perspective?</li></ul>

Now you try it

Using the example above, create a template in your RRS to record information from your research. Use it not only to record the information you are gathering but to reflect on and react to it.

Using AI tools in research

Understanding how to use AI tools appropriately within the extended essay process is an important part of maintaining academic integrity while taking advantage of modern research capabilities. The IB recognises that AI technologies are increasingly a part of academic work, and it does not prohibit their use; rather, it emphasises ethical, transparent and purposeful usage of these tools.

The IB views AI as a tool that can support learning when used properly, not as a replacement for student thinking and work. Just as you might use a calculator for complex calculations in mathematics, AI can serve as an assistant in certain aspects of the research process. However, the extended essay must remain fundamentally your own intellectual work.

AI in the extended essay process

AI tools can be helpful in several phases of your extended essay journey.

Uses of AI in the extended essay process

1 Topic exploration and brainstorming
AI can help generate initial ideas, suggest connections between concepts, or identify dimensions of a topic you might not have considered.

2 Resource discovery
Traditional academic search tools like Google Scholar, JSTOR and your school's library databases remain essential resources. AI-enhanced research tools such as Research Rabbit, Connected Papers and SciSpace can be helpful complements by visualising connections between scholarly works, identifying related papers or suggesting research pathways you might not have discovered through conventional searches.

3 Understanding complex ideas
AI can summarise difficult concepts to help you grasp foundational knowledge before developing your own analysis.

However, AI tools also have limitations that you need to critically evaluate.

AI's blind spots: What to watch for

AI complements but does not replace expertise:
AI can find information but lacks deep understanding and critical judgement that comes from specialised study. Your own thinking and analysis remain essential.

AI misses nuance and context:
AI responds only to what you ask and cannot truly understand subtle contexts or frameworks. The quality of its output depends entirely on the quality of your input.

AI can 'hallucinate':
It may confidently present incorrect information or create false citations. Always verify facts and references from reliable academic sources.

Remember

Your research question should primarily develop through your own exploration, background reading and consultation with your supervisor. You might occasionally consult AI for perspective on how to structure or refine your research question, but this should only happen after substantial personal engagement with your topic. Any AI-generated suggestions should just be one input among many, and must be adapted to reflect your unique interests and understanding.

When using AI tools, remember that this is a partnership where you remain the leader:

- ✓ You are the driver: AI should assist your thinking, not replace it. The insights, analysis and conclusions must be your own.
- ✓ Maintain transparency: Be open with your supervisor about how you are using AI tools in your research process.
- ✓ Discuss AI outputs with your supervisor: Share interesting AI-generated insights with your supervisor during reflection sessions to evaluate their relevance and accuracy together.
- ✓ Prioritise learning: Focus on how AI can deepen your understanding and extend your thinking, rather than using it to bypass the learning process.

The following uses of AI are considered violations of academic integrity:

✗ Having AI write paragraphs, sections or entire drafts of your essay.

✗ Using AI-generated research questions without significant modification and personal input.

✗ Asking AI to create reflections on your behalf.

✗ Using AI to translate your essay from one language to another for submission.

✗ Attempting to hide your use of AI tools.

Citing uses of AI

According to IB guidelines, you must clearly cite AI-generated content in the following scenarios:

- when you directly quote text produced by an AI tool
- when you paraphrase or modify AI-generated content
- when you use AI-generated images, charts or other visual elements.

Your citation should include:

- the name of the AI tool
- the prompt you used
- the date you generated the content
- proper formatting according to your chosen citation style.

There is more information on citation formats for AI tools in Chapter 8.

Remember

At the time of publication, the following research-focused AI tools were available to support your extended essay process. While specific tools will naturally shift and change over time, the principles of using AI ethically as a research assistant remain constant.

- **AI research assistants:** While general chatbots like ChatGPT can help brainstorm, Perplexity.ai is specifically designed for research with built-in citation capabilities.
- **Literature discovery tools:** Elicit and Semantic Scholar can extract data efficiently, helping jumpstart your inquiries by identifying relevant academic papers.
- **Visual mapping tools:** Research Rabbit and Connected Papers create visual maps of related sources, helping you explore academic 'rabbit holes' and create 'playlists' of relevant material to discuss with your supervisor.

Remember that keeping the human at the forefront is paramount. While AI can assist you, there is no substitute for your own critical thinking and collaboration with your supervisor.

Important: Before using any AI tools, you must check your school, district, and country policies regarding AI usage. Regulations vary widely across institutions and regions, and you must comply with all local governance of AI. When in doubt, consult with your extended essay coordinator or supervisor about which tools are permitted in your context.

Organising your research materials

Just as professional researchers maintain meticulous records, you will need a systematic way to organise your scholarly journey. Good organisation not only makes writing easier, it also helps maintain academic integrity.

Activity

Here are some ideas for building your personal research library.

Create a clear structure in your RRS:

- Design a folder system by topics/subtopics.
- Use descriptive, consistent file naming.
- Maintain a master reference list from day one.
- Create backup systems for all materials.
- Document successful search strategies and sources.

For every source you encounter:

- Capture complete citation information immediately.
- Note specific page numbers for potential quotes.
- Record access dates for online materials.
- Save direct URLs or DOIs and download PDFs when possible.
- Document your search journey (terms used, databases searched).

Personal organisation strategies:

- Use the source evaluation template introduced earlier.
- Create multiple entry points to your research (by topic, method, relevance).
- Develop your own visual coding system (colours, symbols, tags).

Example

For her Business Management essay research planning, Amira has created folders for Remote Work Policies, Productivity Metrics and Organisational Culture. Within each of these, she keeps:

- PDF copies of journal articles
- citation details in a master document
- notes linking sources to specific aspects of her research question
- colour-coding to track which sources support different arguments.

Now you try it

Using the ideas above, set up templates for building your own personal research library in your RRS.

Remember

Digital sources can disappear or change, so always save a personal copy of important materials, along with their citation details, including the date you accessed them.

Key takeaways: Chapter 6

- Research is cyclical, not linear. Expect to revisit, rethink and refine your approach throughout the process.
- The quality of your sources matters. Focus on academic sources such as peer-reviewed journals, and avoid unreliable sources like Wikipedia that cannot be verified.
- Organisation is key! Keep systematic notes, folders and citation tracking from day one.
- Engage actively. Do not just read sources, but evaluate, analyse and connect them to your research.
- Use AI wisely, for search and organisation. Never use it for content generation or critical thinking.

Key terms

abstract: a summary of the contents of a piece of academic research

conceptual understanding: a deep comprehension of key ideas, principles and theories, which allows you to make connections across disciplines and apply knowledge to new contexts, rather than merely memorising facts

DOI: (Digital Object Identifier): a unique string of numbers, letters, and symbols assigned to digital content (such as online articles) which provides a permanent link to their location on the internet (since URLs can change or expire)

footnotes: notes printed at the bottom of a page that provide extra information, explanation or references about something that has been mentioned on that page

index: an alphabetised list, found at the end of a book, of key terms, ideas, names and topics covered within that book, along with page numbers where each can be found within the text

jargon: specialised language concerned within a particular subject, culture or profession

plagiarise: the act of using someone else's words or ideas and not crediting them

propaganda: the purposeful distribution of information to help or harm the cause of a government or organisation

synthesise: to combine separate elements into a whole

Chapter 7 – Planning and organising your essay

This chapter covers the following:
- The thesis statement
- Outlining your essay

Learner profile traits
Balanced
Reflective
Open-minded

The thesis statement

As you saw in Chapter 3, your research question is the guiding force of your extended essay. It shapes and focuses your inquiry and sets down what you hope to learn. Your **thesis** statement will provide an arguable answer to your research question. It does not need to use the same language as the research question; in fact, simply turning the research question into a statement will not produce a good thesis statement. Instead, think of it as a more concrete, detailed answer to the question you posed – one that provides a basic 'road map' of how your essay will arrive at that response. Your thesis statement initiates your line of argument, which should flow consistently through your essay, linking your research question to your findings and conclusion.

Characteristics of a strong thesis statement

Like your research question, your thesis should be:

- worded in clear, precise and concise language
- arguable
- focused.

In addition, your thesis statement should:

- present a defensible argument
- offer a hint as to the scope and organisation of the essay to follow
- make clear the importance and worthiness of your topic (think of your reader asking, 'Why does this matter?').

A strong thesis can help you prepare the best organisation for your essay, too. Because the thesis offers a road map for your reader, it also requires you to first determine that route!

Remember

Because your extended essay is a longer paper, your thesis statement can be two sentences rather than one. This is particularly useful if you want to present your general argument along with the focus, topic and other general information in the first sentence, and then provide a more detailed road map in the second.

Example

Here is an example thesis statement:

'While the First World War gave rise to many military technological advancements, the development of mechanised tanks fundamentally transformed modern warfare by breaking the stalemate of trench warfare and establishing armoured mobility as a cornerstone of military strategy. Although aircraft, submarines and chemical weapons also emerged as significant innovations during the war, tanks proved most important by combining firepower, protection and mobility in a way that continues to dominate land warfare a century later.'

This statement presents the argument in the first sentence. The second sentence hints that the writer will discuss other major advancements as well, to demonstrate why they argue that tanks were ultimately the most important innovation.

After you have done a lot of your research, gathered your data or completed your experiment (depending on your subject), you will decide on the answer to your research question. This may be very different from what you thought at the beginning of the process! Remember that an investigative research project such as the extended essay is recursive, so your argument and organisation will probably change, adapt and evolve as you research, outline and write. Remain open-minded and, rather than attempting to force your original argument, allow your research, thinking and reflection to guide your final thesis.

Activity

Take some time to articulate a response to your research question, including the components above. This will be your working thesis statement.

Features of a strong thesis statement

✓ Is it clear? Does my thesis statement use the best, most effective word choice? (Remember – you do not have to use 'big words' for your essay to sound sophisticated and intelligent.) Are there any words that might be made more concrete, precise or straightforward?

✓ Is it analytical? Does my thesis suggest that I will be offering my own interpretation, evaluation, and resolutions rather than merely summarising information?

✓ Is it argumentative? Does my thesis offer an arguable claim that will link my research question, my findings and my conclusions?

✓ Is it relevant? Does my thesis use language appropriate to my subject or subjects and thus make clear my knowledge and understanding of that subject or subjects?

Remember

These questions derive from the elements in Criteria A and C. Criterion A evaluates the framework of your essay, including the research question, but since your thesis is a response to that question, it also applies here. Criterion C assesses your line of argument. Your thesis statement serves as an anchor point that you will return to throughout your essay, threading it through your analysis to create a cohesive pathway that develops your ideas. This sustained line of argument connects your research question, findings and conclusions, allowing readers to follow your thinking process clearly from introduction to conclusion. As with the research process itself, writing is recursive. The thesis you establish at the beginning provides direction, but it also runs through your whole essay, binding it together.

Example

In Chapter 4, you looked at an example of Gerry's Visual Arts and Philosophy interdisciplinary extended essay topic. Now look at the research question and a possible working thesis statement for Gerry's essay.

Research question: 'To what extent did artist Marisol Escobar use postmodern philosophy to challenge the boundaries between high and low art during the 1960s to 1970s?'

Working thesis statement: 'Through her deliberate fusion of folk-art techniques with fine art practices and her ironic commentary on mass culture, Marisol Escobar exemplified postmodern philosophy's challenge to artistic hierarchies, particularly in her wooden sculptures and assemblages from 1962 to 1975, which deliberately blurred the boundaries between "high" and "low" art forms.'

This is a strong thesis statement for the following reasons:

- It is clear: The language is precise, and it gives concrete examples and a period; it also identifies specific philosophical concepts.
- It makes a clear, arguable, original claim.
- It allows for in-depth visual analysis as well as the application of philosophical frameworks.
- It uses appropriate terminology and concepts for the two subjects and subtly relates to the Interdisciplinary framework of 'culture, identity and expression'.

Now you try it

In your RRS, write your working thesis statement. Then, assess it against the checklist above. Put your thesis statement aside for at least a day or two then return to it with fresh eyes and see how it 'stands up'.

Outlining your essay

There is no magic formula for determining when your research phase is complete. As you begin to outline and write, you may find that you need additional information or to take your essay in a slightly different direction. However, once you feel you have a solid understanding of your topic and have formed a tentative argument, you can start to map out your essay.

As you compose your outline, have the extended essay assessment criteria in front of you as a guide, to ensure that you are meeting requirements as you work.

Below are some strategies for turning your working thesis statement and your research notes into an outline for your essay.

Strategy 1

Take your thesis statement apart and identify what information you will need to prove your argument.

Example

Here is an example working thesis statement for Mathilde's Social and Cultural Anthropology topic from Chapter 3:

Research question: 'In what ways and to what extent have Montréal rappers preserved Haitian cultural practices through their music since 2000?'

Working thesis statement: 'Montréal-based rappers of Haitian descent have significantly preserved Haitian cultural practices since 2000 primarily through their use of Creole language, incorporation of traditional Vodou spirituality, and adaptation of Haitian musical elements like rara and konpa, though this preservation has been selective and hybridised with Quebec's contemporary hip-hop culture.'

Based on this thesis, Mathilde will need to do the following in her extended essay:

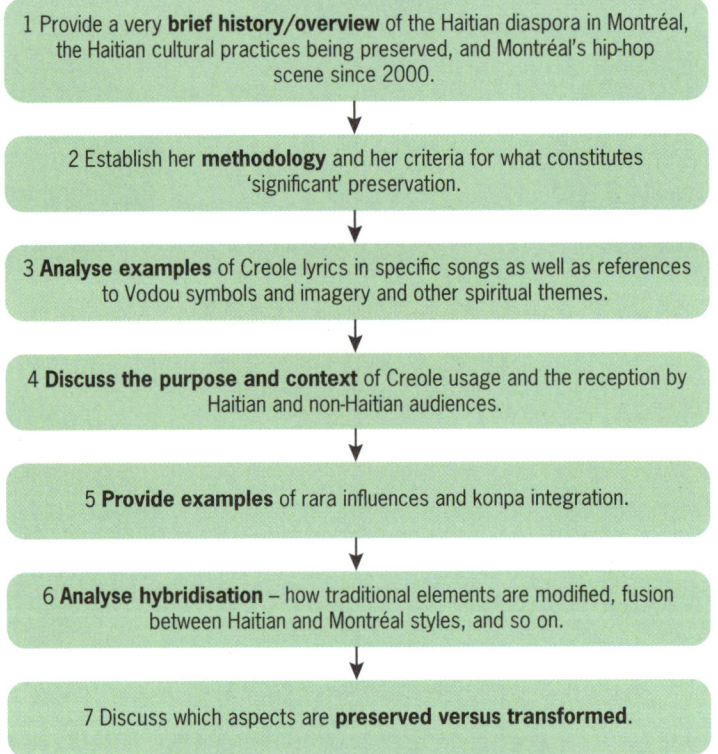

1. Provide a very **brief history/overview** of the Haitian diaspora in Montréal, the Haitian cultural practices being preserved, and Montréal's hip-hop scene since 2000.

2. Establish her **methodology** and her criteria for what constitutes 'significant' preservation.

3. **Analyse examples** of Creole lyrics in specific songs as well as references to Vodou symbols and imagery and other spiritual themes.

4. **Discuss the purpose and context** of Creole usage and the reception by Haitian and non-Haitian audiences.

5. **Provide examples** of rara influences and konpa integration.

6. **Analyse hybridisation** – how traditional elements are modified, fusion between Haitian and Montréal styles, and so on.

7. Discuss which aspects are **preserved versus transformed**.

To satisfy the requirements of the extended essay, Mathilde should also evaluate her own investigation. She should explain its strengths and limitations, and suggest avenues for future research.

Strategy 2

Identify 'chapters' or subsections you feel you will want or need to include to fully discuss your topic and answer your research question. Even if you do not end up including these in your final essay, they can help visually organise your thoughts.

Strategy 3

Look at an example of a high-scoring extended essay in your subject and note how it is organised. Create a 'reverse' outline from the essay. Next to each paragraph, identify what the writer is trying to do. Use different-coloured highlighters to annotate the essay.

- ==Use one colour to mark== where the writer makes a claim.
- ==Use another colour to mark== where the writer uses ==evidence to support that claim== (and whether that evidence is from a primary or secondary source).
- ==Use another colour== where the writer ==analyses== their evidence.
- ==Use another colour where the writer synthesises the research== and brings the argument together in an ==evaluative way==.

<u>Underline</u> wherever you see the writer returning to their thesis or line of argument. Notice how they integrate quotations and evidence, when and where they evaluate their investigation, and where they are using a particular subject-specific methodology or terms.

Crafting a successful extended essay often comes down to a combination of good research, good thinking and good organisation. Consider the following example approach:

1. Introduction
   - Opening statement setting the stage for the discussion
   - Brief explanation and **contextualisation** of the topic and its significance or worthiness
   - Research question
   - Thesis statement

2. Methodology and literature review
   - Explanation of the methodology
   - Review of existing literature on the topic (from both fields, if interdisciplinary)
   - Identification of a gap in scholarship that this essay seeks to address
   - For some essays, it will be helpful to justify the choice of texts being analysed (for example, if pairing two literary works) or the scope of the investigation

3. Body of essay

This will be the bulk of the essay, and its contents will vary based on your subject(s), but here is where you:

   - analyse texts or creative artefacts (for subjects like Literature or Visual Arts)
   - present the experiment and data gathered (for the Sciences)
   - explore and analyse primary sources and secondary scholarship (for Individuals and Societies)
   - include figures and tables that help illustrate a point being made, such as in a Science or Economics essay.

Within body paragraphs, especially for topics in the humanities, you should aim for a balance between claims, evidence and analysis, as well as between primary and secondary sources. Most of the writing should be your own thoughts about the primary sources. If you rely too much on secondary sources to build a discussion, you will not have the opportunity to sufficiently demonstrate your analytical skills.

Whatever subject you are writing about, each of your body paragraphs should focus on a single point, with evidence and analysis to support that point. Body paragraphs should follow a clear line of reasoning and should build upon each other.

4. Discussion and evaluation

    This should conclude the body of the essay.
    - Discuss and synthesise (bring together) your findings.
    - Evaluate the strengths and limitations of your investigation.
    - Address counter-arguments.

5. Conclusion
    - Restate both research question and thesis.
    - Briefly summarise the paper's key findings and reiterate their significance.
    - Suggest avenues for future investigation.

6. Works cited or references
    - Provide full references for sources cited in the essay.

Remember

Effective organisation requires self-management skills, but it saves time (and stress) in the long run. It is easy to become so immersed in your own work that you find it hard to assess it from an outside perspective, as what makes sense to you may not be immediately clear to someone else. Ask someone in your class or your supervisor to look at the order of your paragraphs to see if it makes sense to them.

Now you try it

Choose one or more of the three strategies outlined above and try them out in your RRS. After completing any of these activities, take 10–15 minutes to reflect in your RRS:

- What did you learn about your essay's organisation?
- What changes will you make based on this activity?
- What questions or concerns emerged?
- How might this help with your final essay?

Creating an outline can be hard work! However, if you have a good outline, you will find it much easier to write your essay because you will already have taken the time to think through what can be the most difficult part of essay-writing: organising your thoughts and argument.

Remember to maintain balance by taking time to focus on the whole you. Schedule regular 'brain breaks', engage in physical and/or creative activity, rest and reflect on how this process is helping you build vital skills such as time management, confidence and perseverance!

Remember, too, that your supervisor is always available to review your work and provide guidance. Regular check-ins can help ensure you are on the right track.

Key takeaways: Chapter 7

- A strong thesis statement not only offers a response to your research question, but also establishes the content of your essay and a road map for proving your argument.
- Creating an outline takes work but will make the writing process much easier and will ensure that you are writing a well-organised essay that delivers on the promises made by your thesis and meets the requirements of the extended essay.

Key terms

contextualisation: placing an idea within its relevant background or framework, showing how it fits into the larger picture

thesis: a subject for a discussion or essay

Chapter 8 – Citing and integrating sources

This chapter covers the following:
- The importance of academic citation
- When and how to cite sources
- Integrating sources effectively
- Ensuring academic integrity and ethical research

Learner profile traits
Communicators
Principled

The importance of academic citation

Think of citation as giving credit where credit is due. When you are writing academically, you need to acknowledge the ideas, words and work of others who have contributed to your field of study. It is like creating a map that shows where your ideas came from and how they connect to other people's work.

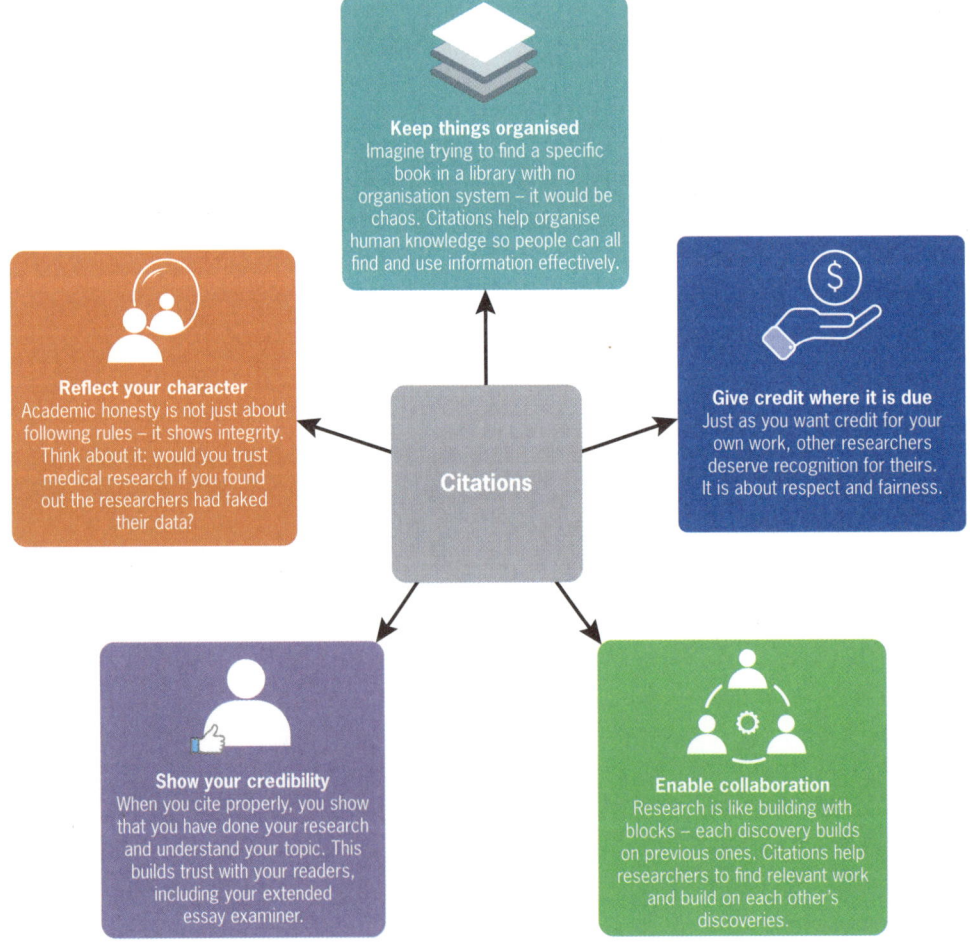

> ## Remember
> Think about your own research experiences.
>
> - How have citations helped you find useful sources?
> - When have you built on someone else's ideas to develop your own thinking?
> - Why do you think academic honesty matters in your field of study?
>
> When you research and write with integrity and honesty, you show yourself to be principled and you demonstrate respect for others' intellectual property rights.

When and how to cite sources

When to cite sources

If you are wondering whether to cite a source, the answer is probably yes! It is better to give a citation and be sure you are writing with integrity than not to give one and risk your work appearing sloppy or unethical. As a rule, whenever you use the ideas, frameworks, theories, methods, data or words of others, you should give them credit by citing them.

When to cite!

- When you use a source's exact words or phrasing. Those words should go in quotation marks to signal that they are not your own.
- When you are using a word or phrase coined by the source.
- When you use an image, diagram, chart, media or creative artefact that is not your own creation.
- When you introduce facts, data or ideas from another source.
- When you are paraphrasing someone else's work. Even if you are using your own words, you must give credit to the original source for the ideas and information.
- When you are using information that is not common knowledge, or when you are unsure whether it would be common knowledge for your reader.
- When you use the framework, theory, method or structure of someone else's work.
- When you have collaborated with someone else.
- When you consult generative AI tools.

How to cite sources

Most disciplines have an established format for citations. This may vary in terms of the information you should include, how it is formatted, and the style of citing within the body of the essay, as well as the list of sources appended to the essay. Some of the most common citation styles are APA, MLA, IEEE, Harvard, Chicago and Turabian. The IBO does not dictate which style you must use, although your school may have guidelines or rules regarding citation styles. If not, it is best to use the citation style with which you are most comfortable, or the style most often used by the subject (or one of the subjects) of your extended essay.

Once you decide on a citation style, make sure you use it consistently and accurately throughout your essay. There are style manuals for each citation style, as well as numerous resources and tools for creating citations. If you do not know about them, your local or school librarian, media specialist or supervisor can direct you to them.

Whichever citation style you choose, there are two key components to proper citation:

- Citation within the body of your essay: The formatting for this depends on the style and may be simply a superscript number, for example, Patel[1], or a number in brackets such as [3], or it may be a longer **parenthetical**, for example (Patel 14).
- Complete source information: Depending on the citation style, this might be found in a footnote, or it may be in an alphabetised list of references at the end of the essay.

Think of this as the process of connecting puzzle pieces. The in-text citation points your reader to the full source information. Without both pieces, your reader cannot trace your research path or verify your sources.

Remember

Cite as you write! Many students fall into the trap of thinking they will add citations later, but this is a bad idea. The extended essay takes months to complete and over that time, you may:

- forget where you found specific information
- forget which words were yours and which came directly from a source
- mix up which ideas came from which sources.

The IB considers *all* these mistakes academic misconduct, whether you commit them by accident or on purpose. Being forgetful or disorganised is no excuse! So, use your RRS. Every time you take notes from a source, make sure you:

- indicate direct quotations with quotation marks; even if you end up paraphrasing the quotation later, doing so will help you remember whose words were whose
- write complete source information
- note page numbers for quotations and key ideas
- add your own thoughts separately.

Integrating sources effectively

Skilfully integrating sources into your essay will make your academic writing more sophisticated. Done correctly, source integration creates a conversation between your ideas and those of others; it strengthens your arguments and demonstrates your engagement with existing knowledge.

Activity

When you want to quote or otherwise cite another source, practise weaving it into your own sentences effectively and in a way that is grammatically correct. Look at the following examples of integrated quotations from an extended essay on the ways that technology has transformed communication, and the commentary on how effective each example is.

Example 1

Social media has changed how people talk to each other. 'The widespread adoption of digital communication platforms has fundamentally altered interpersonal dynamics, leading to decreased face-to-face interaction, the emergence of new linguistic patterns' (Garcia). People communicate differently now.

This is not very effective because it simply drops a long quote in the middle of two sentences.

- The sentence that precedes the quote does not introduce or frame the quote within the broader discussion.
- The sentence that follows the quote does not analyse the quote or explain its significance; it merely summarises without adding new insight.

Example 2

In 'Digital Communication Patterns in the Modern Era', Maria Garcia says, 'The widespread adoption of digital communication platforms has fundamentally altered interpersonal dynamics, leading to decreased face-to-face interaction, the emergence of new linguistic patterns, shifting social norms, and the development of platform-specific communication styles that prioritise brevity and visual elements over traditional verbal expression' (2024, p.45). This quotation shows how social media affects communication. This proves my point about changes in how people communicate.

This is not very effective because, even though it presents the source to introduce the quotation, it does not prepare the reader for why it will be included.

- The quotation is too long – it does not need to be included in its entirety.
- The sentences that follow the quote use awkward wording ('This quote shows') and do not provide much in the way of specific discussion of the quotation (it remains general).
- The text does not explain which parts of the quotation are particularly relevant.

Example 3

The rise of social media has transformed modern communication patterns in subtle but profound ways. Communication researcher Maria Garcia points to a 'fundamental shift in interpersonal dynamics', noting particularly how digital platforms have led to 'the emergence of new linguistic patterns' that favour economy of language and greater emphasis on visual expression (2024, p.45). Such new ways of speaking are inextricably linked to social media patterns of speech.

This is effective because the student embeds key phrases from the source into their own wording and their own argument.

- It uses sophisticated language, such as 'points to' and 'noting', rather than 'this shows' or 'she says'.
- The analysis is woven into the use of the source rather than being 'dropped in' afterwards.
- The student – not the source – is doing the thinking and explaining here.
- The student has actively made the source their own, rather than using it passively, to substitute for their own work.

Now you try it

Find an essay you have written for a Diploma Programme course in which you quoted and cited someone else. This might be an essay for your Language and Literature course, a portion of your History or Psychology IA, or a research paper in another course. Look back at how you integrated your quotations. According to the examples above, how would you rate your ability to weave others' words into your own sentences? Do not worry if you feel you need more practice with this – it is a skill that can be learned by paying attention to how other successful writers do so and using them as mentor texts.

Taking the time to hone this skill as you work on your extended essay will strengthen your communication skills not only in the essay itself but in your essays for all your courses. Indeed, many of the internal and external assessments in your courses include criteria related to your ability to use language in clear, coherent, convincing ways.

Ensuring academic integrity and ethical research

Academic integrity and ethical research practices are fundamental to good scholarship. They demonstrate your commitment to being a principled learner and show respect for other people's work and well-being. Think of ethical research as a four-piece puzzle. Each piece matters, and they all work together.

Academic integrity

Key aspects of academic integrity include:

- Authenticity: Your work must be your own original creation. While you can receive guidance from your supervisor and others, you need to do the research and writing yourself.
- Clear attribution: Your readers must be able to distinguish between your work and the work of others that you have used. This means proper citation of sources and clear indication of quotations.
- Accurate reporting: You must report your research findings and data as fully and accurately as possible. Never falsify or manipulate data to fit what you think it 'should' be.

> ### Remember
>
> If you use generative AI for research, you must be able to verify the information it produced. Generative AI is not peer-reviewed, and it can make mistakes known as 'hallucinations'. For factual claims, historical information, data or academic analysis, you must cite proper scholarly sources.
>
> For example, it would not be advisable to make the following citation:
>
> *The Industrial Revolution fundamentally altered European social structures through the emergence of new urban working classes (ChatGPT, 2025).*
>
> Instead, cite the source of the information:
>
> *The Industrial Revolution fundamentally altered European social structures through the emergence of new urban working classes. (Thompson, 2019, p. 42).*

Transparent AI use in research

The IB requires proper acknowledgment of AI tools in your extended essay. When directly including AI-generated content, cite it both in-text (with prompt and date) and in your bibliography according to your school's citation style. For AI tools that influenced your thinking without being directly quoted, include a brief statement after your conclusion or in your Researcher's Reflection Space (RRS) describing their role (e.g., "ChatGPT was used to help identify potential theoretical frameworks"). The RRS is ideal for including chat histories and documenting how AI shaped your thinking process, ensuring transparency while maintaining the authenticity of your work.

For example:

As part of my research methodology, I utilised ChatGPT to help organise my initial literature search and identify potential connections between theories. All factual information and academic analysis presented in this essay are supported by proper scholarly sources, as cited.

Remember that your extended essay should primarily cite peer-reviewed academic sources, books by recognised scholars, primary sources and other credible academic materials. AI tools should be acknowledged for their role in your process, but they cannot replace proper academic sources for factual information or scholarly analysis. There is more comprehensive guidance on the ethical use of AI in your extended essay research process in Chapter 6.

Appropriate uses of AI:	Inappropriate uses of AI:
✓ to help brainstorm ideas and refine your thinking	✗ to write any portion of your essay that you then present as your own work
✓ to use visual mapping tools to find sources	✗ to generate a complete essay
✓ to compare and evaluate other source materials	✗ to use AI outputs without citing them as a source
✓ to assist with basic tasks like checking spelling and punctuation	✗ to translate your essay into another language and submitting the translation as if you had written it in that language originally
	✗ to rely solely on AI-generated content without verifying it against other sources

Remember

The field of generative AI is evolving, so it is best to stay up-to-date with IB's latest guidance through their Academic Integrity and Effective Citing and Referencing Guides, which your teachers and supervisors can access through the IB Programme Resource Centre.

Well-being

Some research topics may be sensitive or challenging for you or others involved in your research. If you are working on a potentially sensitive topic, discuss this with your supervisor, who can help you approach the subject responsibly and appropriately. Remember that your research should respect privacy, cultural contexts and individual perspectives – for example, medical confidentiality, socioeconomic sensitivity when conducting research among peers, or dealing with religious beliefs.

Safety

You should always consider the safety and comfort of everyone involved in your research. If it involves other people, you must obtain their **informed consent** and protect their privacy. For research involving experiments or **fieldwork**, particularly in sciences, there are specific safety guidelines. Your supervisor can provide these, and you must follow them carefully.

Environment

Consider how your research process might affect the environment. If you are conducting fieldwork, be careful not to disturb natural habitats or ecosystems. Think about sustainable choices in your research process, from your use of paper and materials to your modes of travel for research. Small choices can make a significant difference in reducing your environmental impact.

Good practices for ethical research

- ✓ Keep detailed records of your sources in your RRS.
- ✓ Cite as you write rather than trying to add citations later.
- ✓ Be clear about what help you have received from others.
- ✓ When in doubt about whether to cite something, cite it.
- ✓ Ask your supervisor if you are unsure about any ethical issues.
- ✓ Consider the impact of your research on others and the environment.
- ✓ Follow all safety guidelines carefully.
- ✓ Make sustainable choices where possible.

Remember

Ethical research practices protect both you and others. If you are unsure about any ethical aspects of your research, always consult your supervisor. They can provide access to detailed IB guidelines that will help you make appropriate choices.

Key takeaways: Chapter 8

- Citation is fundamentally about giving credit where it is due and showing how your ideas connect to and build upon other people's work. It helps you organise knowledge, demonstrates credibility and reflects academic integrity.
- Every citation needs two parts: an in-text reference and complete source information.
- When in doubt about whether to cite something, do so! It is better to cite more than you need to than to risk academic misconduct. This includes citing AI tools if you use them in your research process.
- Do not just drop in quotes; integrate sources smoothly into your writing.
- Research ethics extends beyond citation to include participant well-being, environmental impact and responsible AI use.

Key terms

fieldwork: investigations or search for material or data in a real, natural environment rather than in school, work or laboratory

informed consent: permission given by someone who understands fully what they are agreeing to

parenthetical: referring to something that is written or said in addition to the main part of what you are saying, or information found inside a set of parentheses such as an in-text citation

Chapter 9 – Structuring your essay

This chapter covers the following:
- The structure of your extended essay
- Practice exercises for writing your essay
- Additional features for an interdisciplinary essay

Learner profile traits
Communicators
Thinkers
Knowledgeable

The structure of your extended essay

There are two aspects to consider regarding the structure of your essay:
- The formal IB requirements that govern how your essay should be presented and formatted – these are the technical rules you need to follow for submission.
- The academic structure – how you organise your ideas, arguments and evidence to effectively communicate your research.

Both types of structure are essential for success.

Whether you have chosen a single-subject or interdisciplinary pathway, your extended essay should follow the general academic structure outlined on the following pages:

- Introduction
- Body of the essay
- Conclusion

For each of these sections, explained below, you will see a list of the key components and an explanation of how they are evaluated by the assessment criteria.

Introduction

For some essays, one or two paragraphs will be enough to introduce your research question and note the context, worthiness and thesis. However, it is fine if you need several paragraphs for your introduction.

Below is an example of a structure for an introductory section to an extended essay that requires more than one paragraph. In fact, the term 'introduction' here is fluid because, depending on your subject(s), your **methods** and methodology (the research approaches, frameworks, and strategies used in a particular discipline) might be more detailed and thus require their own section following the introduction. For example, an extended essay in the sciences will probably involve more detail on the design and execution of the experiment. This includes aspects such as variable control, replication protocols, statistical analysis methods, and equipment specifications. It may also contain a more extensive literature review that examines previous related studies, theoretical frameworks, and established methodologies. In contrast, a Literature essay would likely have a different focus.

Content	Assessment criteria
<ul><li>Research question</li><li>Research methods (how you are gathering your data – the tools you are using)</li><li>Methodology (your overall approach, lens or theoretical framework – the strategy for choosing and using those tools)</li><li>Thesis statement and signposting of your essay's structure</li><li>Relevant background and context (keep this information brief, just a few sentences will do)</li><li>Clear justification of the worthiness and originality of the research question and, for an interdisciplinary pathway, of the choice of an interdisciplinary approach and selected subjects</li><li>Brief 'literature review' of the existing research and scholarship on your topic (which makes clear that you understand your essay is part of a larger scholarly conversation)</li></ul>	<ul><li>A: Framework for the essay (the research question and methods provide an effective framework for the essay)</li><li>B: Knowledge and understanding (of relevant and appropriate concepts, terminology and existing scholarship in your subject or subjects)</li><li>C: Analysis and line of argument (your thesis will begin to signpost your line of argument and its analysis)</li></ul>

Example

Subject: IB Geography

Research question: 'To what extent have economic and social factors driven rural exodus in China, and what are the resulting impacts on the social fabric, economic viability and cultural preservation of rural communities?'

Sample text	Commentary
In recent decades, China's meteoric economic rise has not only transformed its urban landscapes, it has also fundamentally altered the demographic of its rural communities. As millions of working-age people migrate to expanding cities in search of economic opportunities, vast areas of China's countryside face an unprecedented challenge: severe depopulation. This phenomenon, characterised by the exodus of young people and the subsequent ageing of remaining populations, represents one of the most significant demographic shifts in modern Chinese history.	The opening paragraph sets the stage (context and location) and engages the reader's interest by presenting a topic with clear significance. Assessment criteria:<ul><li>A: Establishes an appropriate focus for an IB Geography essay.</li><li>B: Displays excellent knowledge and understanding of the concepts and terminology of IB Geography.</li></ul>
The scale of rural depopulation in China is staggering. According to China's National Bureau of Statistics, the rural population decreased from approximately 790 million in 1990 to 510 million	This paragraph provides a concrete statistic and connects it to less quantifiable issues such as the shifting social fabric. It also continues to establish the worthiness of the topic.

Sample text	Commentary
in 2020, representing a decline of nearly 36% ('Communiqué'). Behind these numbers lie several different social, economic and political factors that together have contributed to this dramatic transformation of rural China's demographic landscape.	Assessment criteria: • A: This paragraph makes clear the significance and relevance of the topic. • B: The paragraph continues to display excellent knowledge and understanding of the concepts and terminology of IB Geography.
This extended essay aims to investigate the multifaceted causes and far-reaching consequences of rural depopulation in China, with a particular focus on the period between 1990 and 2020. By examining this phenomenon through both economic and sociological lenses, this research seeks to answer a fundamental question: To what extent have economic and social factors driven rural exodus in China, and what are the resulting impacts on the social fabric, economic viability and cultural preservation of rural communities? To do so, this investigation will draw upon a diverse range of sources, including government statistics, academic research, ethnographic studies and policy documents, to construct a comprehensive analysis of rural depopulation. By synthesising quantitative data with qualitative insights from case studies of specific rural communities, this essay aims to provide a nuanced understanding of both the macro-level trends and micro-level impacts of this demographic transformation. This investigation argues that while China's rapid urbanisation and economic modernisation have contributed to rural depopulation through uneven regional development and wage disparities, the consequences extend far beyond economic metrics, fundamentally threatening rural communities' social structures, cultural heritage and long-term sustainability.	This paragraph clearly states a focused research question and establishes the research methods and methodology that will be used to answer the question. Assessment criteria: • A: The paragraph states the research question, method and methodology. • B: The above factors also reveal knowledge and understanding of relevant and appropriate concepts, terminology and the methods typical of the subject. • C: The paragraph offers a thesis statement and a roadmap of the essay structure.
The significance of this research extends beyond mere demographic analysis. As China attempts to deal with the challenges of food security, preserving cultural heritage and ensuring balanced regional development, understanding the dynamics of rural depopulation becomes crucial for policymakers and scholars alike. Moreover, China's experience offers valuable insights for other developing nations facing similar rural-urban migration patterns.	These two paragraphs emphasise the worthiness of the topic and situate it within the larger scholarly conversation, continuing to satisfy the requirements of Criteria A, B and C.

Sample text	Commentary
Through this research, I hope to contribute to the broader academic discourse on urbanisation, rural development and demographic change in contemporary China, while also exploring potential solutions to mitigate the negative impacts of rural depopulation on affected communities.	

Body of the essay

Most of your essay will be body paragraphs. This is where you build a focused, reasoned argument based on your investigation and your analysis of the information, data and any evidence you have gathered. Depending on your selected subject(s), the structure and format of your body paragraphs may vary, but the following guidelines apply to all essays. If your introduction did not mention methods, methodology, brief background/context, or a review of current scholarly literature, you should include those in the early body paragraphs.

Content	Assessment criteria
Distinct paragraphs, each of which features: • a **topic sentence** with a single focus • presentation of findings, data and observations • analysis and evaluation of data or source material • clear relevance to your line of argument • a balanced combination of claims, evidence and analysis/discussion of how the evidence supports the claim. Body paragraphs should: • build upon each other • remain focused on the essay's line of argument • transition clearly and logically, using either transition/signal words or connections between ideas. Body paragraphs may be grouped using chapter headings or subheadings, as appropriate. Many body paragraphs will integrate the work of other scholars to support the argument, provide counterclaims, offer space for new ideas, and so on. Body paragraphs that evaluate methods and materials may occur at the end of the discussion and offer suggestions for future studies.	• A: Framework for the essay (the essay should follow the appropriate structure for the subject(s) you have chosen). • B: Knowledge and understanding (of relevant and appropriate concepts, terminology, existing scholarship in your subject(s)). • C: Analysis and line of argument (this section of the essay should consist primarily of your own thoughts, interpretations and analyses). • D: Discussion and evaluation (explain the significance of your findings and support your claims with appropriate and convincing evidence; offer a range of perspectives; evaluate your research methods, materials and findings – their strengths and limitations).

Example

Subject: IB Dance

Research question: 'To what extent has classical Indian dance influenced the development of modern European ballet techniques and choreography from 1900 to 1975?'

This paragraph builds on a preceding discussion, and offers an example of the point being made about influential figures in modern ballet whose work was shaped by Indian dance, particularly in terms of storytelling.

Sample text	Commentary
The influence of classical Indian dance on storytelling in European modern ballet becomes particularly evident when examining the revolutionary work and impact of Ruth St. Denis in the early 20th century. After encountering Indian dance forms during her travels, St. Denis incorporated elements of Bharatanatyam's precise footwork and mudras (hand gestures) into her choreography, notably in her 1906 piece 'Radha' (Singh 22), as can be seen in Figs. 3 and 4. Here, the dancer's pose is similar to the hand and footwork of Bharatanatyam in the use of Asamyuta hasta mudras, particularly the pataka and Katakamukha. In addition, her torso bend and the Araimundi position of the feet derive from Bharatanatyam (Singh 16). All of these movements are helping tell the story of the dance - here, the milkmaid Radha's emotion upon leaving Krishna. St. Denis further explored these influences in her 1911 work 'Cobra', where she combined Indian-inspired arm movements with ballet's turning sequences, creating a unique fusion that challenged Western dance conventions of the time. As can be seen in Figs. 5-7, at key moments of the ballet 'St. Denis would curve her wrists inward while extending her fingers like lotus petals, a direct reference to Indian hastas' (hand positions). During the piece's climax, she would 'rise from a deep plié while her arms moved in hypnotic waves, her fingers alternating between traditional Indian pataka [flat palm] and ballet's soft port de bras' (Clarence). Thus, this new style broke away from traditional ballet's stiff, upright positions by adding more floor-based movements and meaningful hand gestures. Moreover, the impact of this influence extended beyond St. Denis's own work through her influence on Martha Graham, who studied at Denishawn School. Graham's development of modern	- The paragraph includes a topic sentence with a single focus tied to the line of argument. (A: Framework) - The discussion uses concrete evidence and examples, which are discussed and analysed. (B: Knowledge and understanding; C: Analysis and line of argument) - The writer weaves secondary sources into their own sentences fluidly and effectively. - This paragraph makes clear its connection to the line of argument and it offers an example of the larger focus of this part of the essay, which are particularly influential figures influenced by Indian dance who then shared that influence with others.

> **Sample text**
>
> dance technique, particularly 'her focus on the torso as the centre of expression', is very similar to the core principles of Kathak and Bharatanatyam, where movement originates from the spine (Jones 71). This technical innovation ultimately filtered into contemporary ballet choreography. Jared Lopez argues that this influence can be seen in the works of Maurice Béjart, whose 1975 piece 'Bhakti' explicitly merged classical Indian dance's rhythmic complexity with ballet's classical vocabulary (23-24). Because of St. Denis' chain of influence, the influence of Indian dance's focus on telling stories through movement, opened up new ways for modern European ballet to express itself.

Example

Subject: IB Literature and IB Psychology

Research question: 'To what extent do domestic pressures contribute to female psychological deterioration in Euripides' *Medea* (431 BC) and Gillian Flynn's *Gone Girl* (2012), and how do these works, despite their historical separation, present parallel critiques of the psychological impact of gender expectations on women?'

This body paragraph focuses on evaluating an interdisciplinary essay's methods, strengths and limitations.

Sample text	Commentary
While this investigation effectively establishes parallels between Medea's and Amy Dunne's psychological deterioration within their domestic spheres, certain limitations must be acknowledged. The analysis relies heavily on feminist literary theory, particularly Betty Friedan's concept of 'the problem that has no name' which, while helpful, may oversimplify the complex contexts of Ancient Greece and modern America. A broader theoretical framework incorporating historical perspectives on women's roles in Ancient Greek society could have provided deeper insights into Medea's actions. Additionally, the investigation might have benefited from examining a wider range of contemporary psychological research on domestic pressure and mental health, which could have strengthened the connections drawn between societal expectations and	This paragraph displays the writer's ability to: - evaluate their investigation and offer avenues for future research - assess the strengths and limitations of their methodology and theoretical frameworks - explore the effect of approaching the topic from an interdisciplinary standpoint. (D: Discussion and evaluation)

Sample text

psychological breakdown. The comparison between these texts, separated by more than two millennia, also raises questions about the universality of female experience that could have been more thoroughly addressed. Despite these limitations, the investigation's focus on close textual analysis of specific scenes where domestic pressures manifest in violent thoughts or actions has yielded valuable insights into how both authors portray the relationship between domesticity and psychological stability. In addition, the consideration of real-world psychological studies of the same issue has helped illuminate the psychological state of each protagonist. Future study might explore the limitations of fiction on the understanding of psychological conditions.

Conclusion

The conclusion to your extended essay may be two paragraphs, depending on your subject and topic.

Content	Assessment criteria
- A return to the research question - Synthesis/review/summary of the discussion - Completion of the line of argument by connection to broader context/implications, showing relevance beyond the specific topic.	- A: Framework (structure – including a thoughtful, meaningful conclusion) - B: Knowledge and understanding (demonstrate a careful analysis of research to develop a deep understanding of the topic) - C: Line of argument (the conclusion should feel like the natural endpoint of this line)

Example

Subject: IB History

Research question: 'To what extent did the implementation of the Marshall Plan in Italy between 1948 and 1952 worsen regional economic disparities between the industrial north and rural south?'

Sample text	Commentary
This investigation of the Marshall Plan's implementation in Italy (1948–1952) demonstrates that economic aid alone did not drive Italy's post-war recovery. Rather, the evidence suggests that the Plan's success stemmed from its integration with domestic political reforms and social programmes,	This conclusion: - summarises the analysis and reiterates the topic's significance (A: Framework/structure – a thoughtful, meaningful conclusion)

Sample text	Commentary
particularly in the industrial north. The analysis of previously overlooked regional economic data reveals significant disparities in aid distribution, with northern regions receiving 48% more per capita funding than the south, as noted above. While American diplomatic records portray the Plan as purely economic assistance, Italian government archives suggest it was deliberately used to strengthen anti-communist political forces, especially in industrial centres. These findings challenge traditional interpretations that emphasise the Plan's economic rather than political impact. This investigation thus contributes to our understanding of how international aid programmes can both solve and create domestic challenges, while highlighting the importance of examining economic policies through both political and social lenses.	- makes clear a deep understanding of the topic and subject (B: Knowledge and understanding)
- leaves the reader with a sense of the essay's usefulness to future study and an end to the line of argument (C: Line of argument)
- includes a final summation of the investigation's findings and their significance (D: Discussion and evaluation).

Practice exercises for writing your essay

The following exercises are designed to help you craft thoughtful, organised paragraphs.

Please only choose one or two of the activities below and complete them in your RRS.

Activity

Introduction: Background exercise

List everything your reader needs to know about your topic.

Rank each point from 1–3:

- 1 = Essential context
- 2 = Helpful but not crucial
- 3 = Interesting but maybe too detailed

Keep only the 1s and strongest 2s for your introduction.

Read your working introduction to a subject teacher. Ask them if you are including too much or too little information.

Remember

Do not fall into the trap of reporting rather than analysing! Limit your background and context sections to the essentials. There is more information on making sure you analyse rather than summarise in Chapter 10.

Activity

Introduction: 'Opener' exercise

Write three different opening sentences, trying each style:

- Surprising statistic: Find a shocking number related to your topic.
- Scenario: Paint a brief scene that illustrates the problem.
- Contrast: Present opposing views or situations.
- Quote: Find a meaningful, intriguing quotation from one of your primary or secondary sources.

Read each of these aloud and pick the most engaging one. Also, reread the opening sentences of some of your secondary sources (such as journal articles) and use them as exemplars.

Activity

Introduction: Building a bridge

Write your 'opener' at the top.

Write your research question and thesis at the bottom.

Fill the gap by answering these questions:

- What context does my reader need?
- Why is this issue important now?
- Who is affected by this problem? Each answer should flow naturally into the next.

Activity

Body: Evaluating evidence

Create a T-chart.

On the left, list all pieces of evidence you have found that relate to a claim you wish to make.

On the right, rate each piece from 1–5 using these questions:

- Is it from a reliable source?
- How recent is it?
- How directly does it support your point?

Only use evidence scoring 12+ points in your paragraph.

Activity

Body: Evidence 'sandwich'

Choose one strong piece of evidence you found in your investigation or from a secondary source.

Write three different lead-in sentences introducing that evidence.

Write three different follow-up sentences explaining the evidence's significance.

Mix and match to find the strongest combination.

Activity

Body: Backwards paragraphing

Start with your conclusion (what you want to prove to your reader), then work backwards by asking:

- What evidence proves this point?
- What background does my reader need first?
- What is the clearest order for presenting these ideas?

Draft the paragraph following your outline.

Activity

Conclusion: Completing the circle

Use this **mnemonic** to brainstorm concluding sentences. You will need some notecards and blank paper.

Collect the major points you made in your essay body (key claims, arguments, and so on) on separate notecards.

Identify connections between these major points – lay the notecards out in a circle around a piece of blank paper, and then draw lines and arrows on the paper which identify patterns or relationships between the points that you might not have stated in your essay.

Revisit your research question on another blank sheet of paper and write 2–3 new sentences that answer your question. Try to use different words and phrases than you have used already in your essay.

Consider limitations – below the research question and your answers, be honest about what your essay or research did not include and why that might matter (you may already have addressed these limitations in the body of your essay).

Link your topic to larger contexts – try to explain how your essay connects to studies in your subject or subjects and how it fits within the larger scholarly conversation on the topic.

Emphasise your essay's significance – below the context reflections, explain why a reader – especially one in your subject or subjects – should read your essay. Why does it matter?

Once you have completed the 'CIRCLE' activities, you should have plenty of material for a meaningful conclusion!

Now you try it

Remember, you only need to choose one or two of the activities above to complete in your RRS. Return to them throughout the writing process. Later, you can transfer any really good ideas you have created here into your actual essay document.

After writing each of your paragraphs, ask yourself the following questions and revise any for which the answer is 'No'.

- ✓ Does my topic sentence clearly state the paragraph's main idea?
- ✓ Have I included at least one or two pieces of credible evidence (for body paragraphs)?
- ✓ Did I explain how each piece of evidence supports my point (for body paragraphs)?
- ✓ Are my citations formatted correctly?
- ✓ Does the paragraph flow logically from point to point?

Additional features for an interdisciplinary essay

So far, this chapter applies to both single-subject and interdisciplinary essays. However, there are some additional considerations for an interdisciplinary essay:

- Your introduction should make clear why you paired your selected subjects and how they enable the most effective consideration of the topic.
- Your body paragraphs should 'prove' the claims above. While you do not need to explicitly justify your use of the two subjects in all your body paragraphs, your discussion and analysis should themselves demonstrate, in a natural, organic way, that approaching your topic through the two subjects makes the most sense.
- You will also need to demonstrate excellent knowledge and understanding of the relevant concepts and terminology of both subjects. As you saw in Chapter 5, when writing an interdisciplinary extended essay, you do not need to give equal weight to both subjects. The research question and topic will naturally determine how much you draw from each subject area. However, it is important to show how combining elements from both subjects helped you answer your research question more effectively than using just one subject would have done.

Key takeaways: Chapter 9

- The extended essay should follow a clear three-part structure: introduction (with research question, methods and context); body (with evidence-based analysis); conclusion (synthesising findings and addressing broader implications).
- Body paragraphs should each have a clear focus, with topic sentences, relevant evidence, analysis of how evidence supports claims and logical transitions between paragraphs.
- The assessment criteria shape each section.
  - The introduction establishes framework (Criterion A), shows subject knowledge (B) and previews argument (C).
  - The body paragraphs demonstrate knowledge and understanding (B), analysis (C) and evaluation (D).
  - The conclusion synthesises discussion (A) and (C).
- For interdisciplinary essays, explain and demonstrate through analysis why combining two subjects provides better insight than using just one subject.

Key terms

method: a specific procedure, technique or way of doing something (the 'what' and 'how' of the research project); this is distinct from methodology, which is the general reasoning behind the methods chosen and the overarching approach (the 'why')

mnemonic: a learning technique to help you remember important elements, often by creating an acronym (an abbreviation using the first letter of each word)

topic sentence: the main sentence in a paragraph that presents the central idea of that paragraph

Chapter 10 – Writing your essay

This chapter covers the following:
- How to begin writing
- Using the assessment criteria
- General guidelines for effective academic writing
- Analysis and evaluation
- Academic diction and tone

Learner profile traits
Balanced
Thinkers
Communicators
Open-minded

How to begin writing

It can feel like a big step to finally sit down and start writing your essay, but remember – by this stage you have already done much of the hard work. You have:

- crafted a good research question
- read widely in your background research
- read in depth once you settled on a focused topic
- actively engaged with your data, object(s) of study or artefacts, as well as with your secondary sources, identifying your own thoughts and reactions as you worked
- mapped out a rudimentary outline as you organised your thoughts.

Now it is time to put everything together. Bear in mind the following:

- The extended essay process is designed to help you learn – not just about your topic, but also about the research and writing process, and about yourself.
- The IB does not expect perfection. The assessment criteria reward you for what you do well, rather than penalising you for mistakes. That is why the criteria use a 'best fit', holistic approach to grading.
- You have done this kind of writing before, albeit in shorter essays. Your internal assessments (IAs) and the other research and writing assignments in your Diploma Programme all require the same key skills as the extended essay: reading, critical thinking, synthesising sources and analysing.

Remember
Your extended essay topic allows you to consider a larger topic or question, and to include more data and more secondary sources, but the process, skills and outcomes are similar to those you have used in other writing.

TOP TIPS FOR ESSAY WRITING

 Break the task up into small, manageable 'chunks'

Do not try to write the whole essay – or even half of it – in one sitting! Create a writing schedule in which you plan out sections of the essay. You could plan to write one section of the body of the essay one day, your introduction on another day, and so on. Or you may decide you want to set a goal of 300 words (or one page) each sitting. If you end up writing more, even better! If you are struggling one day, give yourself a break and come back to the essay later.

Start where you feel comfortable!

Do not feel you have to begin at the beginning. Sometimes, a rough introduction is enough to get you started, and then you can return later and craft a 'real' one. Begin working on the section of your essay that you feel most interested in or confident about.

 Use different 'thinking muscles'

Print out your research and other notes and physically lay them all out. Spend some time arranging them and writing by hand to create connections and generate ideas. Sometimes stepping away from the computer screen can help reenergise your thinking.

Consider starting to write before you are sure about your argument. You may not know what you really think until you write – and by writing you will clarify your thoughts and recognise new ideas. You may get to the end of a page or section and think, 'Ah, so that's what I really want to argue!' Sometimes what you think is a good conclusion is a much clearer, more refined introduction, with a slightly different focus or argument. Remember: the research and writing process is recursive and does not always proceed in a straight line. Remain open-minded!

Write to learn

 Find good examples

Consult high-scoring papers in your subject or subjects and use them as exemplars in terms of organisation and analysis.

Trying to perfect each sentence as you write will only slow you down. Write without stopping or self-editing, knowing that you can refine your writing later, once you have your ideas down on paper or on screen.

Do not edit or limit yourself as you write your rough draft

 Change your surroundings

Sometimes, working in a different location to normal can help reset your brain and bring new perspective and energy.

As much as possible, remove distractions such as your phone, the internet or anything else that reduces your ability to concentrate and to work efficiently.

Focus!

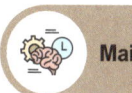 **Maintain balance**

Schedule time to write, but also schedule time to take breaks, give yourself small rewards or do something that allows your brain to rest. Not working may seem counterproductive, but creating balance by allowing yourself time off actually increases your efficiency and productivity, as well as helping to take care of the whole you.

Remember

Because the writing process can take a long time, it is vital to create and stick to a schedule. As you saw in Chapter 2, you should work backwards from the deadlines given to you by your school and allow yourself plenty of time – more than you might think necessary – to do your writing. The tips above assume that you are giving yourself plenty of time to be flexible with the process.

Activity

The following activity can help you begin writing or restart if you get stuck. It is designed to help you gather ideas, start putting pen to paper, find new perspectives or regain motivation or energy.

1. Select five 'writing zones'

Select from any of the following locations:

   At home
   - Bedroom desk (early morning or late evening writing)
   - Kitchen/dining table (when it is clear)
   - Quiet corner of another room
   - Outside or near a window
   - On the floor, set up with pillows

   At school (during free periods/after school)
   - Library
   - Cafeteria during quiet times
   - Study hall
   - Outdoor lunch tables

   In your community (weekends/after school)
   - Public library
   - Local café (if you can buy a drink or snack)
   - Community centre
   - Park bench on nice days

2. Using 5–7 different-coloured index cards:

Write one 'chunk' on each (adapt as necessary to fit your topic and subject).

   - Yellow: Topic brainstorm and research notes
   - Pink: Introduction ideas
   - Blue: First body section + evidence
   - Green: Second body section + evidence
   - Purple: Third body section + evidence
   - Orange: Discussion and evaluation
   - White: Analytical observations

3. Each day, pick *one* zone and *one* card

Based on:

   - where you can actually go that day
   - how much time you have (30–45 minutes is ideal)
   - what type of writing you need to do (a busy café might be great for brainstorming but not great for detailed analysis)
   - your energy level.

4. Rules

Follow these rules:

   - Bring only what you need for that chunk.
   - No phone or other distractions while you are working.

- Work for 30–45 minutes using *just* the one index card and your research notes. It is even better if you can work on paper rather than a computer.
- If one spot works well, it is okay to return there.
- Have a backup spot in mind (in case library is full, café is too loud, and so on).

Now you try it

In your RRS, set up everything you need to start using the process in the activity above. Follow it as you begin the writing process.

Remember:

- Match your location to your task (quiet spots for complex thinking, livelier places for brainstorming).
- Bring headphones for unpredictably noisy places.
- Check operating hours before planning to use community spaces.
- Have a weather backup plan for outdoor spots.
- Keep your materials organised in a folder or large envelope so you can grab and go.
- You can also do this 'writing journey' only at home, by working in 30-minute chunks and simply changing locations there!

Using the assessment criteria

Rather than consulting the assessment criteria when you have finished writing, use them throughout the process to inform your writing. Examiners read your essay with the assessment criteria to hand, so it makes sense for you to have them in front of you as you write. The five criteria are:

- Criterion A: Framework for the essay (6 marks)
- Criterion B: Knowledge and understanding (6 marks)
- Criterion C: Analysis and line of argument (6 marks)
- Criterion D: Discussion and evaluation (8 marks)
- Criterion E: Reflection (4 marks)

Read and reread the general assessment criteria, making sure that you understand what is being evaluated. The extended essay subject-specific guidance explains how the assessment criteria are interpreted for each subject in a section called 'Considering the assessment criteria'. Here, you will find explanations of how to demonstrate, for example, the 'knowledge and understanding' of Criterion B or to successfully 'discuss and evaluate' (Criterion D) in a particular subject.

General guidelines for effective academic writing

There are a few standard rules and techniques that apply to all academic writing, regardless of subject. Knowing and understanding these will enable you to write a sophisticated, effective extended essay.

Paragraphing

Each paragraph of your extended essay should:

- have a single focus that you make clear in a topic sentence – this is a kind of mini thesis statement for the paragraph, which may need several points in support of its general idea
- develop the essay's overall line of argument by building on what came before and setting up what comes next
- include one or more claims or points that develop the specific message of this paragraph
- support the claim(s) with relevant evidence (such as data, quotations, facts and examples)
- explain/elaborate on the evidence to demonstrate how it proves the claim(s).

Remember

A topic sentence:

- is usually the first sentence of a paragraph
- introduces what the entire paragraph will be about
- acts like a mini thesis for the paragraph
- does not make a specific claim but rather presents an overview of the subject of the entire paragraph
- sets the stage.

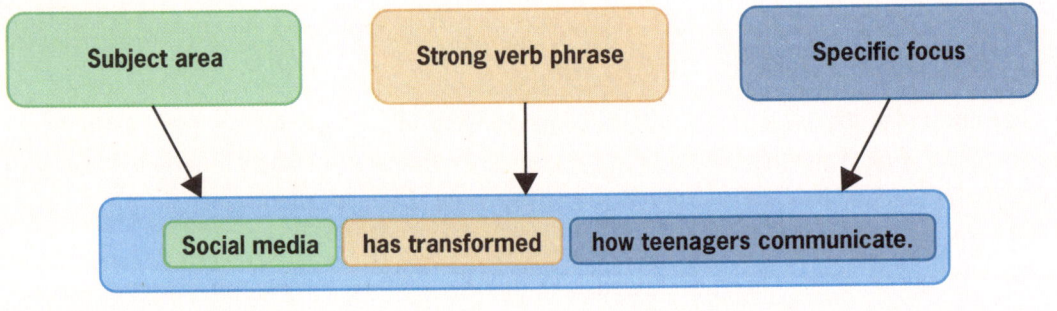

Remember

A point:

- is the specific argument or claim you are making
- can be stated within or right after the topic sentence
- directly states your position on the topic.

For example, this sentence could follow the topic sentence above: 'The shift to digital communication has made teenagers less comfortable with face-to-face interactions.'

Using effective transitions

One of the ways you can keep your reader engaged and ensure effective, logical development of your line of argument is to use transitions. These can be indicated by words or phrases.

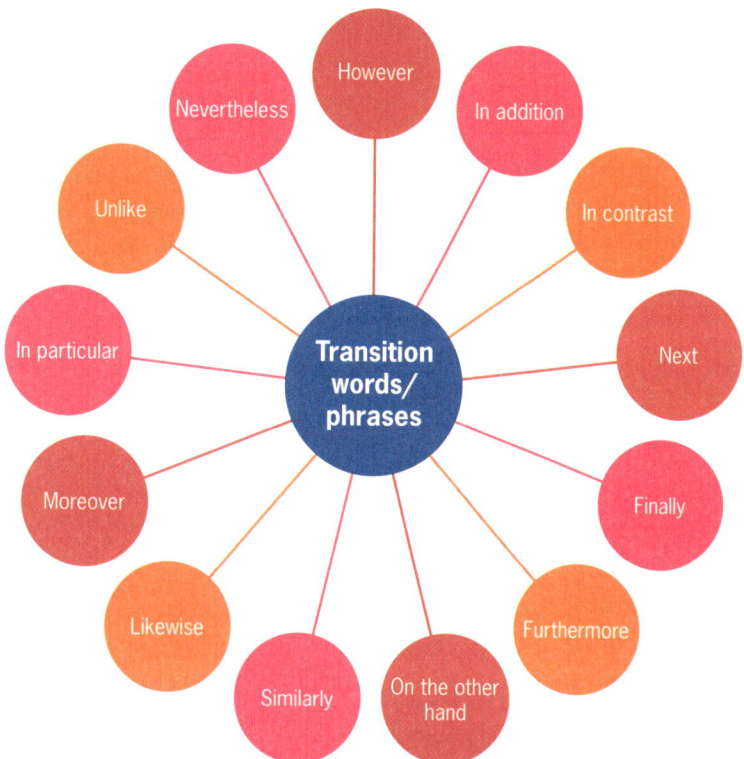

Transitions can also be indicated through the careful linking of concepts or relationships between ideas. For example, you could link the content of different paragraphs by:

- identifying a relationship, such as cause in one paragraph and effect in the next
- progressing chronologically
- comparing and contrasting a single sub-topic or element
- echoing terms or concepts from earlier paragraphs in a new context
- stacking evidence by providing increasingly compelling arguments to support your main point
- using the last sentence of a paragraph to set up the first sentence of the next one
- explaining how one paragraph builds upon, extends, or offers an alternative to the previous paragraph.

Good transitions do not only help your essay flow well, they also make it easier for an examiner to see your continued focus on and development of your line of argument (assessed in Criterion C).

When you have finished writing your essay, print it out if you can, and cut out each paragraph. They should connect with each other and flow logically so someone else should be able to reconstruct your essay from the individual paragraphs, like fitting pieces of a puzzle!

Analysis and evaluation

The extended essay assessment criteria distinguish between analysis (Criterion C) and evaluation (Criterion D). Analysis involves examining evidence to produce relevant findings and develop your line of argument. Evaluation involves discussing the significance of those findings and assessing the strengths and limitations of your research. This section focuses mainly on analytical writing, but both skills are essential for a successful essay.

Analysis vs. evaluation

Analysis (Criterion C)

Breaking down information to:

- Interpret evidence
- Identify patterns and relationships
- Explain connections
- Support claims with evidence

Analysis questions:

- What patterns do I see in my findings?
- How does this evidence support my point?
- Why is this connection significant?

Example phrases:

'This evidence demonstrates …'
'This pattern suggests …'

Evaluation (Criterion D)

Making judgments about:

- Significance of findings
- Strengths and limitations of methods
- Alternative perspectives
- Broader implications

Evaluation questions:

- Why are these findings important?
- What are the strengths/limitations?
- What different interpretations exist?

Example phrases:

'These findings are significant because …'
'A limitation of this approach is …'

In Chapters 3 and 4, you learned how to craft an analytical research question – that is, a question that leads to analysis rather than summary or description. A strong research question will make it easier to write analytical paragraphs. However, be careful not to stray into description or reporting as you write your body paragraphs. There are several reasons that this happens:

- You may be unsure of the difference between analysis and summary.
- You may be in a hurry, so you summarise because it is faster and easier to do that than to deeply engage with and think through the material.
- You may be uncomfortable with or unsure about the information.
- You may assume the reader understands what the evidence means.

To ensure that you are analysing, imagine your reader asking, after every point you make, 'Why?' and 'So what?' or 'How does this relate to your overall point?'

You can also check you have written analytically by looking at each point you have made and writing a sentence after it that begins, 'This matters because …' or 'This shows …'. Finish those sentences. (You can remove those stems in your actual essay because what will follow should be able to stand on its own. For example, you can remove 'This shows that' from this sentence without losing impact: 'This shows that young people are much less comfortable with face-to-face interactions than their parents are.') Then, cross out most of what comes before them to eliminate anything that is not analysis.

Example

Look at this example from a Global Politics essay.

Initial paragraph: India has increased its naval presence in the Indian Ocean region. Many island nations, such as the Maldives and Sri Lanka, have signed maritime agreements. These deals include port access and joint patrols. Some countries are shifting their partnerships from China to India.

Add 'This shows ...' or 'This matters because ...' after each statement:

- India has increased its naval presence in the Indian Ocean region. *This shows* how emerging powers can project influence without aggressive military action.
- Many island nations, such as the Maldives and Sri Lanka, have signed maritime agreements. *This matters because* these small island nations are strategically located along crucial maritime trade routes.
- These deals include port access and joint patrols. *This shows* how India is creating a network of friendly ports to establish itself as the region's primary security partner.
- Some countries are shifting their partnerships from China to India. *This matters because* it demonstrates how smaller nations are reevaluating their diplomatic alignments based on geographic and cultural proximity.

Delete or minimise the pure description, keeping the statements that follow 'This shows ...' or 'This matters because ...'. Begin connecting them. For example, you might combine the above and end up with this paragraph:

India's expansion of naval presence demonstrates how emerging powers can project influence through diplomatic means rather than military pressure. The strategic targeting of island nations reveals India's broader aim to secure crucial maritime trade routes. By establishing a network of friendly ports, India transforms geographic proximity into diplomatic leverage. The shifting alignments of smaller nations from China to India illustrates the growing importance of cultural and historical ties in regional security partnerships.

Then, develop these analytical points further by asking 'So what?' Doing so will force you to think through your argument more deeply and should yield a more sophisticated discussion. Remember to remain open-minded as new thoughts and revisions occur, rather than sticking to a preconceived argument.

A final version might read like this:

India's naval cooperation across the Indian Ocean shows how emerging powers can establish regional dominance through 'soft' maritime diplomacy instead of military force. Joint patrols and port agreements serve as strategic measures against external influence in what India considers its maritime territory. By becoming the primary security partner for smaller island nations, India converts its geographical position into diplomatic advantage, creating a buffer zone against competing powers. Providing naval assistance to states previously aligned with China demonstrates how India uses its democratic identity and trade history to present itself as a preferable regional partner. This strengthens India's position as the leader of Indian Ocean security, while highlighting the balance smaller states must maintain between regional powers.

Now you try it

Using the example above as a guide, check and then develop a paragraph from your own essay.

- Copy one of your body paragraphs into your RRS, leaving space between each statement.
- Add 'This shows ...' or 'This matters because ...' after each statement (if the statement is not already followed by an explanation or elaboration).
- Delete or minimise the pure description, keeping the 'because' and 'shows' statements. Begin connecting them.
- Ask the 'so what' and 'why does this matter' questions of each statement.
- Revise the paragraph accordingly.

Remember

The sample above demonstrates effective analysis – breaking down information and explaining its significance to support a claim. For evaluation (Criterion D), you would also need to:

- discuss the broader significance of these findings
- consider alternative interpretations
- assess strengths and limitations of your research approach
- explain implications beyond your specific example.

Effective evaluation often appears in your discussion sections and conclusion.

Now you try it

Practise distinguishing between analysis and evaluation. Choose a paragraph from your draft essay that contains evidence or data. First, write an analytical follow-up that:

- explains what patterns or relationships you see in the evidence
- shows how this evidence supports your specific point
- makes connections to your research question.

Then, write an evaluative follow-up that:

- discusses why these findings are significant in your field
- considers alternative interpretations or perspectives
- addresses any limitations in your evidence or approach
- suggests broader implications of your findings.

Compare your two follow-ups. Notice how analysis focuses on interpreting the evidence itself, while evaluation places it in a broader context and assesses its value.

Avoiding unnecessary reporting or summary

Avoid summarising or retelling information that the reader does not need. You can assume that your reader is familiar with your topic, so you only need to include a summary of relevant information to establish the context for your essay (such as a one or two sentence overview of a novel you are discussing in a literature essay). It is also helpful to tailor what you mention in that summary to the topic at hand. In other words, if you provide a brief overview of a historical event, do so in a way that also mentions the information that is relevant to your topic.

Example

Below are two sample summaries of *The Great Gatsby* in a literature extended essay comparing how Fitzgerald's novel *The Great Gatsby* (1925) and Albert Camus' *The Stranger* (1942) explore themes of isolation and the hollowness of social façades.

Here is a poor example:

The Great Gatsby, F. Scott Fitzgerald's masterpiece published in 1925, tells the story of the mysterious self-made millionaire Jay Gatsby, who throws extravagant, glamorous parties every weekend at his fancy mansion in the wealthy Long Island community of West Egg. Gatsby, who made his fortune through questionable means during Prohibition, is hopelessly in love with the beautiful and wealthy Daisy Buchanan, whom he met years ago when he was a poor soldier, but who is now married to the rich but deceitful Tom Buchanan from an established East Egg family. The entire story unfolds through the observant eyes of Nick Carraway, Daisy's cousin, who conveniently moves into the modest cottage next door to Gatsby's mansion. Throughout one memorable summer of 1922, Nick becomes increasingly involved in the drama as he witnesses Gatsby's elaborate attempts to reconnect with and win back Daisy, a goal that eventually leads to a series of tragic events involving Myrtle Wilson, whom Tom has a relationship with, her mechanic husband George, and culminating in Gatsby's shocking death in his own swimming pool while waiting for a phone call from Daisy that never comes.

There are several issues with this summary:

- It is too long (the essay must fully discuss both novels in 4,000 words).
- It could apply to any analysis of the novel, rather than focusing on the essay's thesis.
- It prioritises plot over argument, spending valuable words on unnecessary detail ('glamorous parties', 'modest cottage', 'phone call that never comes') rather than establishing the novel's deeper significance.
- It includes unnecessary background information.
- It reads like a book report or review rather than setting up an analytical argument – notice how much space is devoted to simply narrating events chronologically.
- It fails to target the specific analytical purpose. If the essay wants to compare *Gatsby* to *The Stranger*, none of these details establishes the key parallels about social conformity, identity and moral judgement that need to be explored.

Now look at this improved version:

Told through the eyes of narrator Nick Carraway, *The Great Gatsby* follows the tragic story of Jay Gatsby, a self-made millionaire whose carefully constructed identity and extravagant lifestyle mask his desperate attempt to win back his lost love Daisy Buchanan, now married to old-money aristocrat Tom. The novel explores the emptiness beneath the glittering facade of 1920s American society as Gatsby's pursuit ends in disillusionment and death.

This summary is good for the following reasons.

- It covers key plot points.
- It avoids unnecessary details (like the specific location of West Egg or the mechanics of Gatsby's parties) that would not serve the comparison.
- It implicitly sets up the parallel with Meursault (in Camus' novel) as narrator/observer.
- It established the social dynamics that both novels critique.
- It points to the key difference with Meursault (who refuses to construct a false identity).
- It highlights both novels' concern with social authenticity.

Thus, the summary reminds the reader about crucial information in the novel but also uses every detail to serve the argument the essay is building, not just tell the story.

Academic diction and tone

There are a few easy ways to make your essay more sophisticated and engaging. The first is to make sure you proofread your work carefully to check for correct capitalisation, punctuation and grammar (see Chapter 11). You should also consider your language choices carefully, using precise, meaningful words.

Verbs

The following diagrams outline weak or vague verbs and then offer clearer, more vivid examples.

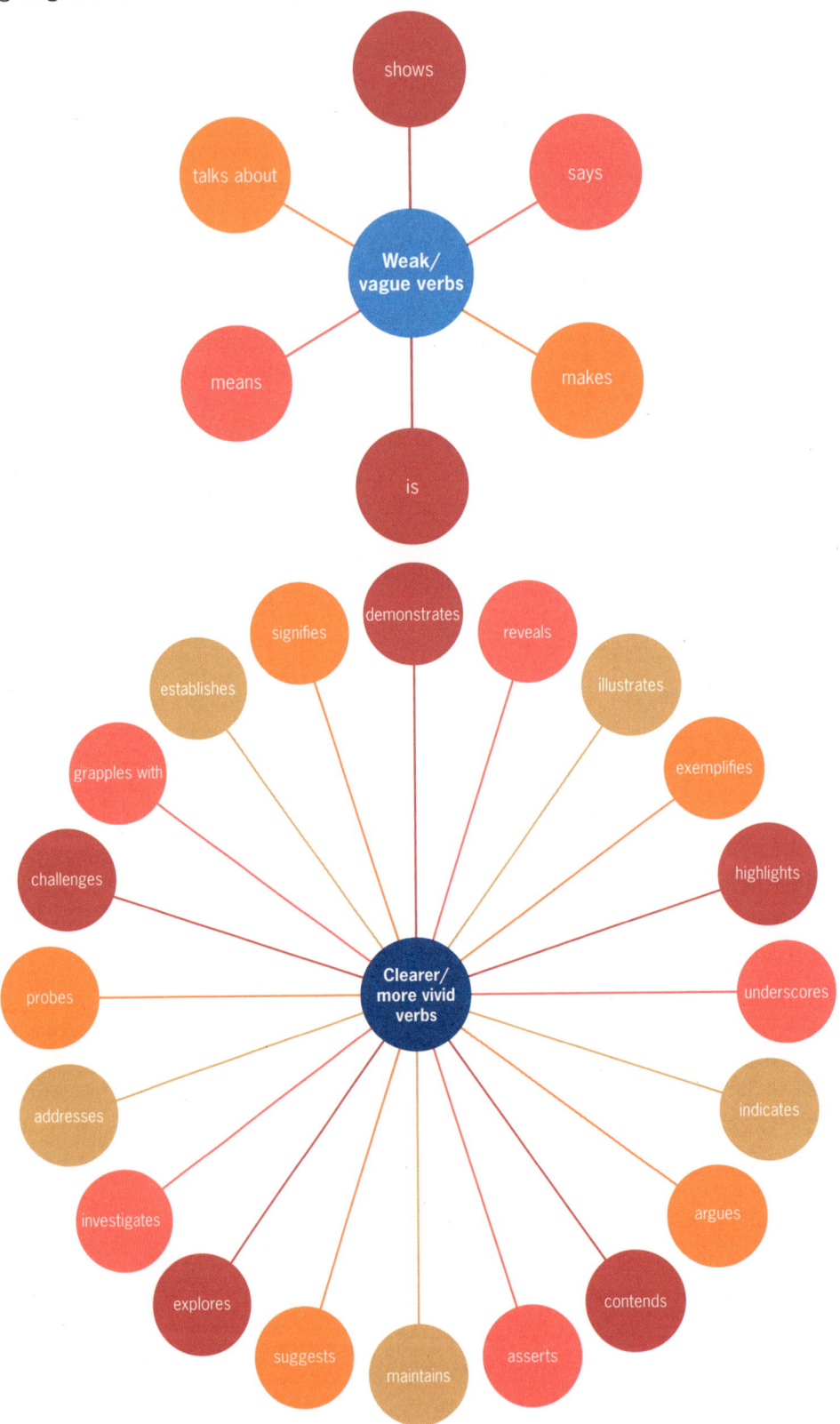

Descriptors and nouns

The following diagrams outline weak or vague descriptors and clearer, more vivid examples.

Personal pronouns

Avoid personal pronouns. Using 'I' is not necessarily forbidden in formal essays, but in most cases its use can be avoided without losing meaning. You do not need to say, 'I think' – since you are making the claim, the reader already knows it is your opinion. Your reader already knows that what you are about to say is your thought.

For example, look at this sentence:

I believe that Shakespeare's use of dramatic irony in Macbeth creates tension throughout the play.

Now look at it without the words 'I believe that':

Shakespeare's use of dramatic irony in Macbeth creates tension throughout the play.

Not only is the second statement just as clear, it is also more compelling. By removing the 'I' you are making the idea feel like it exists on its own rather than being merely your opinion.

> ### Remember
> 'I' is rarely used in academic writing. You are establishing yourself as a scholar, so the tone of your essay should be formal and polished. Your reflective statement, however, offers a space for your personal opinions, feelings and thoughts (see Chapter 12). It is an ideal place to present your own voice as you walk your examiner through your personal growth as a researcher and writer.

A similar issue arises when responding to a research or **rhetorical question** with a simple 'yes' or 'no', such as this response to a History essay research question:

Yes, the Industrial Revolution fundamentally altered European social structures, as evidenced by the emergence of new urban working classes and the decline of traditional craftsmen.

Here, the use of a direct 'yes' or 'no' is unnecessary, as this statement shows:

The Industrial Revolution fundamentally altered European social structures, as evidenced by the emergence of new urban working classes and the decline of traditional craftsmen.

> ### Now you try it
> Read through any parts of the essay you have written so far and check them for vocabulary and sentence structure that detracts from your work's sophistication. Look for places where you may:
>
> - have done too much summarising or describing, or places of summary that could benefit from tailoring to connect to your focus a bit more
> - need to more clearly connect to your line of argument
> - have used tired, vague, or imprecise diction
> - add more evidence, explanation, elaboration, interpretation or evaluation.
>
> Reread the assessment criteria (both general and subject-specific) and ensure that what you have written so far satisfies or exceeds the requirements of each criterion.

Key takeaways: Chapter 10

- You can do this! Make things easier for yourself by creating and sticking to a schedule, and by breaking the writing process into manageable chunks.
- As you write, focus on analysis rather than description by asking 'Why?' and 'So what?' after making claims, and always explain how your evidence supports your points.
- Maintain a formal academic tone by using precise vocabulary, avoiding phrases like 'I think', and removing unnecessary 'yes/no' responses to research questions.
- Structure paragraphs with clear topic sentences, supported claims, and logical connections between them.
- Use the assessment criteria to guide your writing from the beginning, not just at the end, consulting both general and subject-specific guidance.

Key term

rhetorical question: a question designed to make a point rather than to get an answer

Chapter 11 – Revising, editing and presenting your essay

This chapter covers the following:
- The importance of reviewing your rough draft
- Revising your essay
- Editing and proofreading
- The structure, style and layout of a formal academic essay
- IB guidelines for the extended essay presentation

Learner profile traits
Principled
Caring

The importance of reviewing your rough draft

Once you have completed a rough draft of your essay, you will meet with your supervisor to discuss what is going well and where you might clarify or rethink parts of your writing. Remember, when writing your rough draft, you should have focused on getting all your thoughts, ideas and arguments down on paper. Now, you need to **revise** it – see if any of your ideas need to be reviewed or reworked, and improve the fluency and sophistication of your writing. Your supervisor can discuss and provide comments on one draft, but they cannot directly **edit** your work or provide detailed corrections. The revisions you make are your responsibility. So, give yourself time and space to engage with what you have produced and work carefully to maximise your essay's clarity, coherence and effectiveness.

> **Remember**
>
> Try not to get too attached to your rough draft! Revision sometimes requires rewriting, so it may be tempting to just make minor edits. However, think of all the work you have put in to get to this stage. You owe it to yourself to make your essay the best it can be.

Revising your essay

The terms 'revise' and 'edit' are often used interchangeably, but they are two different – although equally important – processes.

Revising

- ✓ Focuses on the 'big picture'.
- ✓ Evaluates the strength and clarity of your overall argument.
- ✓ Assesses the effectiveness of your choice and use of evidence.
- ✓ Looks at your introduction and conclusion to ensure they are relevant, accurate and effective now that your entire argument has been communicated.
- ✓ Re-examines the organisation and flow of your essay to confirm that the order and arrangement of your sentences and paragraphs makes the most sense.
- ✓ Ensures that your line of argument remains focused and solid throughout.

Editing

- ✓ **Proofreads** for smaller details such as grammar, spelling and punctuation.
- ✓ Ensures that your word choice is the clearest and most effective.
- ✓ Confirms correct citation of all sources.
- ✓ Checks formatting and presentation correctness.

It is best to revise first and then edit, as there is not much sense in finessing your style and sentence structure until the broader content is exactly what you want.

How to revise your essay

Follow these steps to revise your essay.

1 Print your draft (or have it open on your computer).

2 Remove all distractions Allow yourself a good chunk of time for this first review – say, an hour.

3 Read your draft aloud
Note:
- the flow of your line of argument (are there places you seem to stray from the focus?)
- the order of your points (does any part seem like it might make more sense if it were moved?)
- your introduction and conclusion (do they make sense, with the body of your essay now in front of mind and all together?)
- paragraph development (are there any parts that feel too long or that might benefit from more information, explanation or evidence? Do you treat each point adequately?)

4 Create a quick outline from the full text of your essay
Try to:
- quickly identify the point of each paragraph and confirm that each paragraph remains focused on one point
- explain how it connects to your line of argument. If it is difficult to identify either of these in any paragraph, make some notes on how you might fix it.

5 'Colour-mark' your essay
This four-step process ensures it aligns with the assessment criteria.
Step 1: Use four colours to highlight key components in each body paragraph.
- Claims: Highlight each time you make a clear argument.
- Evidence: Highlight supporting examples, quotes or data.
- Analysis: Highlight where you interpret or explain how the evidence supports the claim.
- Evaluation: Highlight where you assess the strengths, weaknesses or significance of evidence or perspectives.
Add a star next to any place where you refer back to your thesis or line of argument.
(For digital annotation, use colour-marking tools to achieve the same effect.)
Step 2: Check for analysis and evaluation. Analysis explains the significance of the evidence, explores patterns and connects ideas. Evaluation assesses reliability, limitations and the impact of the argument. Ask yourself: Does my essay contain both, or is one missing? If I have claims and evidence but little evaluation, where can I strengthen my argument?
Step 3: Compare your colour-marked draft with the IB assessment criteria.
- Criterion A (Framework for the essay): Do my paragraphs remain clearly focused on my line of argument? Am I making clear and accurate use of suitable research methods for my subject(s)?
- Criterion B (Knowledge and understanding): Do I use a range of relevant sources and concepts? Am I using subject-specific terminology and concepts effectively to demonstrate my knowledge and understanding?
- Criterion C (Analysis and line of argument): Does my analysis consistently produce relevant findings related to my research question? Have I developed a clear, logical line of argument connecting my research question, findings and conclusions? Is my argument sustained throughout the essay, with each section building upon the previous one to create a cohesive whole?
- Criterion D (Discussion and evaluation): Does my discussion present a balanced view of the significance of my findings, considering both strengths and limitations? Have I provided specific, appropriate evidence to support each claim? Have I connected my findings to the broader context while avoiding unsupported generalisations?
Step 4: Revise your draft.
- Add analysis if evidence is present but unexplained.
- Strengthen evaluation if arguments lack depth.
- Ensure each body paragraph includes claims, evidence, analysis and evaluation.
- Write a brief reflection in your RRS identifying patterns and next steps.

6 Make notes in your RRS about the steps needed to revise this content The more detailed you can be, the better – especially if you can note down why you need to make certain changes.

7 Put the draft away for at least a day

8 Print out another copy of your draft (or have the revised version open on your computer).

9 Repeat Repeat at least some of these 'revisioning' steps once more before finalising your essay.

Now you try it

Use the process above to begin revising your essay for broad-level issues like content, evidence and analysis, organisation and adherence to the assessment criteria. Do not forget to use your RRS to record what you need to do and what you have realised about your essay as a result of this process of revision.

Remember

To make sure that you are analysing rather than describing or summarising, when you see a piece of evidence, ask yourself if you can see the 'So what?'. Have you made it clear why this evidence is included and how it supports your point? Alternatively, look for places where you:

- identify patterns or connections between ideas
- evaluate and interpret data or elements of your sources
- discuss cause and effect
- explain how something works
- offer ideas about the meaning or significance of a piece of evidence.

These are all signs that you are analysing rather than describing or summarising.

Editing and proofreading

When you are happy with the content, it is time to proofread your essay – this will be your final check. The longer you can wait between completing your revisions and doing a final proofread, the better, as it can be difficult to spot errors or inconsistencies if you are still immersed in it. Fresh eyes are always useful.

Remember

When you read silently and quickly, your brain may do something called 'predictive reading'. This is when you *expect* to see a word or phrase, so even if it is not there, your brain adds it in. Your brain may also correct words that are spelt wrong without you noticing. For example: 'Tihs snetecne is treribley mislpeled, but you can raed it.' Your brain untangles the words so you can still understand the sentence. Here is another example: 'When we finished our examination, we went to the beach in order to see our friends, play games and swim in the the sea.' Did you spot the repeated 'the' at the end?

Activity

There are different ways to proofread your essay. You can use some or all these ideas.

- Read your essay aloud slowly, a few paragraphs at a time. Reading every word before speaking it out loud will help you to notice if a word is missing or if you have accidentally included an extra word. It will also help you identify over-long sentences or too much repetition of particular words.
- Print out your essay and read it on paper. Just as reading aloud can help you spot 'invisible' errors, so can reading in a different format. Use a blank sheet of paper to cover all the lines below the line you are reading. This will slow down your reading and make sure you are not reading predictively.

- Read several times, each for a different purpose. For example, on one read-through circle all the punctuation marks in order to ensure that they are used correctly. On another read-through, pay attention only to font type, size and spacing in order to ensure they are consistent.
- Save your essay as a PDF, which is the file format you use for your submission to IB. Print out the PDF so that you make sure that saving in a different format has not caused any awkward page or line breaks, shifted the position of text, images or figures, or revealed any formatting inconsistencies.

Now you try it

- Set your final essay aside for a few days, then come back to it and try some of the proofreading activities above.

The structure, style and layout of a formal academic essay

Think of your extended essay as your ambassador. It will be assessed by someone who does not know you, and you will not be there to explain or defend your ideas. So, your essay must stand on its own merits, making your case clearly and confidently. You can make a good first impression by ensuring that your extended essay is error-free, neat and organised, and that it follows the **conventions** and expectations of an academic paper.

Essay presentation checklist

- ✓ Title page
- ✓ Contents page
- ✓ Numbered pages
- ✓ Correct spacing
- ✓ Clear, legible graphics and figures
- ✓ Correct use of grammar and punctuation
- ✓ Consistency in spacing, font and font size
- ✓ Reference list or bibliography

Remember

Submitting a clean, clear copy of your essay makes it easier for the person assessing it to focus on the content of your essay, trusting that you are a principled, caring, credible scholar working to professional standards.

IB guidelines for the extended essay presentation

The following table contains the IB's requirements for the format of your essay.

Feature	Guidelines
General	- No more than 4,000 words - 12-point font size - 1.5 line spacing - Page numbers beginning with the first page after the contents page - No identifying marks anywhere in the essay (your name, your supervisor's name, your school or institution's name, and so on) - File size no larger than 10 MB (if you have high-resolution graphics in your essay or other embedded images, you may need to condense them)
Title page	- Your student code - Your research question - Title (optional) - Subject-focused or interdisciplinary essay stating the Diploma Programme subject of your essay (such as Psychology or Visual Arts) or the interdisciplinary subjects and the framework it connects to - Word count (if your essay includes footnotes with anything other than citation information, include the following clarification: 'the stated word count includes explanatory footnotes')
Table of contents	- Should reflect the subsections of your essay - If you wrote explicit subheadings in your essay, use those in your table of contents - If you did write explicit subheadings, consider creating some to reflect the content of your essay – enough to give your reader a sense of the essay's organisation and a preview of its contents
Essay itself	- Introduction (page numbering begins on the first page of the introduction) - Body - Conclusion
Works cited or References	- Page name depends on the citation style you chose
Included in the word count	- Introduction - Main body - Conclusion - Quotations - Footnotes and/or endnotes that are not references
Not included in the word count	- Contents page - Headers - Maps, charts, diagrams, annotated illustrations - Tables - Equations, formulas and calculations - Citations/references (whether parenthetical, numbered, footnotes or endnotes) - Bibliography - Reflection and progress form
Appendices	- If applicable, might include material such as a copy of a survey distributed to gather data in a science essay, or the complete text of poems discussed in a literature essay, if they are not commonly accessible - Note that examiners are not required to read any appendices, so anything that is intended as part of your essay should be in the body of the essay itself

These examples are intended to show layout and formatting of an extended essay using the MLA citation style; they are not meant as examples of extended essay writing.

Example: Title page

Student code: 115762

Natural Language Processing
versus
Traditional Analysis:

A Comparative Study of Metaphor Recognition in
Ocean Vuong's Poetry

Research Question:
To what extent do Natural Language Processing algorithms interpret and analyse metaphors in contemporary poetry, such as that of Ocean Vuong, better than traditional literary analysis methods?

Interdisciplinary Extended Essay
Subjects: Computer Science and Studies in Language and Literature
Interdisciplinary framework: Evidence, measurement, innovation
Word count: 3,972

Example: Contents page

Table of contents

Introduction 1
   Ocean Vuong's contemporary poetry
   Natural Language Processing algorithms
Literary analysis methods
   Background and context 2
Methodology and scope
Poem analyses 3
   'Aubade with Burning City' 5
   'Essay on Craft' 7
   'Eurydice' 9
Comparative analysis and assessment 11
Discussion and evaluation... 13
Conclusion 14
Works cited 15
Appendix: full text of poems 16

Example: First essay page

Introduction

The intersection of artificial intelligence and literary analysis represents one of the most intriguing new fields in the humanities. As Natural Language Processing (NLP) algorithms improve and develop, readers may wonder about using them for literary analysis but this raises important questions about the nature of interpretation and even the future of literary criticism. This investigation examines the extent to which NLP algorithms can effectively interpret and analyse metaphors in contemporary poetry, specifically focusing on the complex work of Ocean Vuong, in comparison to traditional literary analysis methods.

Understanding a writer's use of metaphors is something that may seem like it cannot be done by a machine because often it requires understanding of the writer's cultural context, emotions, and the 'grey areas' of language. Traditional literary analysis approaches metaphor through close reading, contextual understanding, and interpretation based on historical, cultural and other frameworks. However, recent advances in NLP, particularly in areas such as language analysis and pattern recognition, have begun to challenge this assumption. Modern NLP algorithms can now identify metaphorical language like a human would; it can recognise patterns across large bodies of text and even attempt to interpret metaphorical meaning through contextual analysis.

Ocean Vuong's poetry provides an ideal testing ground for comparing these two approaches, the human and the machine. His work, particularly in collections like 'Night Sky with Exit Wounds' and 'Time Is a Mother', uses metaphors that are deeply personal and culturally specific, yet universal in their emotional significance. Vuong's metaphors often layer multiple meanings, drawing from his experiences as a Vietnamese American, his family's refugee history, and themes of identity, sexuality, and loss. Thus his poetry can pose both a challenge and an opportunity to evaluate the capabilities and limitations of NLP algorithms in metaphor analysis, while also examining the strengths and potential blind spots of traditional literary analysis methods.

1

Example: Works cited

Works cited

Bryan, Jared A. 'Metaphor Recognition and Interpretation in Natural Language Processing: Recent Advances and Future Directions.' *Journal of Technological Research*, vol. 45, no. 2, 2023, pp. 178–203.

Chen, Wei-Te, and Mohammed J. Zaki. 'DeepMetaphor: A Deep Learning Framework for Metaphor Detection and Interpretation.' *Proceedings of the 60th Annual Meeting of the Association for Computational Linguistics*, 2024, pp. 1205–1220.

Do, Thi Nhu. 'Ocean Vuong's Poetry: Trauma, Memory, and Metaphorical Language.' *Contemporary Literature Review*, vol. 38, no. 4, 2023, pp. 412–428.

Lakoff, George, and Mark Johnson. *Metaphors We Live By: Updated Perspectives in Cognitive Linguistics*. University of Chicago Press, 2003.

Liu, Sarah, and James Martinez. 'Comparing Human and Machine Interpretation of Contemporary Poetry: A Case Study.' *Digital Humanities Quarterly*, vol. 15, no. 2, 2024, pp. 45–67.

Vuong, Ocean. 'Aubade with Burning City.' *Poetry Foundation*, February 2014, https://www.poetryfoundation.org/poetrymagazine/poems/56769/aubade-with-burning-city. Accessed 12 January 2024.

Vuong, Ocean. 'On Earth We're Briefly Gorgeous: The Role of Metaphor in Contemporary Poetry.' *Poetry Foundation Quarterly*, Dec 2014, vol. 89, no. 4, 2023, pp. 12–28.

Zhang, Yi. 'Machine Learning Approaches to Metaphor Detection in Multilingual Poetry.' *International Journal of Digital Humanities*, vol. 5, no. 1, 2023, pp. 89–112.

15

Key takeaways: Chapter 11

- Revision tackles big-picture elements, while editing handles surface details. Always revise first, then edit.
- Effective revision requires distance and fresh perspective, including systematic review of arguments, evidence and analysis.
- Multiple focused read-throughs are essential: check flow, outline for structure and assess against the extended essay criteria.
- *You* own the revision process. While your supervisor can guide you, success depends on your time and effort.
- The format and presentation of your extended essay create an important first impression. Proper spacing, consistent fonts and clear organisation help establish your credibility as a scholar.
- Effective proofreading requires specific strategies, such as reading aloud and checking printed versions.
- Make sure you follow the formatting requirements of the IB extended essay, such as 12-point font size, 1.5 line spacing and lack of any identifying information.

Key terms

conventions: agreed-upon rules for writing (such as grammar, punctuation, formatting and spelling)

edit: to correct errors and improve clarity at the sentence level (such as grammar, spelling and formatting)

proofread: to check a piece of writing before submission, looking for any remaining errors or typos

revise: to rethink and restructure content at a broader level (reorganise ideas, strengthen arguments, and so on)

Chapter 12 – Supervisor meetings and the reflective statement

This chapter covers the following:
- The supervisor's role
- Meetings with your supervisor
- The reflective statement and why it matters
- Planning and writing your reflective statement

Learner profile traits
Reflective
Thinkers
Caring
Communicators
Balanced

The supervisor's role

While the extended essay process is directed and managed by you, your supervisor is there to support you. Throughout the process, they can:

- offer advice or clarification
- help locate sources
- talk through ideas
- give feedback on your work and on your rough draft
- help you think through and overcome questions or difficulties
- encourage you and celebrate progress
- direct you to other sources of help
- confirm the authenticity of your work.

> **Remember**
>
> Your supervisor can ensure you have all the necessary resources and materials, including the extended essay guide, support documents and sample essays. It is important to keep your supervisor informed about your progress, as they play a key role in authenticating your work before it is submitted to the IB for scoring. By verifying that the essay is your own to the best of their knowledge, they help uphold academic integrity.

Your supervisor is also responsible for documenting the three formal meetings that are required as part of the process (see below), authenticating your work and offering summative comments on you as a learner, which are recorded on the RPF.

However, *you* need to take responsibility for seeking help, arranging meetings and keeping to schedule. The more you communicate and remain in regular contact with your supervisor, the better off you will be.

You will not only feel comfortable seeking help when needed, but your supervisor will get to know you, which will help them support you more effectively.

Meeting with your supervisor

The IB requires three separate, formal meetings with your supervisor during the essay planning and writing process. However, it also recommends that you undertake as many meetings and conversations as you and your supervisor decide you need.

Check-ins versus formal meetings

As you journey through the process, you may wish to check in frequently with your supervisor to discuss issues such as:

- thinking through your research question
- understanding appropriate methods and methodology in your subject(s)
- finding or evaluating sources
- outlining, organising or drafting
- motivation, time management and organisation.

In addition to this, you and your supervisor must meet formally three times – at the beginning, middle and end of the process. Specific timeframes for these meetings will be assigned by your extended essay coordinator. Each of these meetings will take 20–30 minutes and they serve three key purposes:

- They help you and your supervisor develop a working relationship (especially if you are not meeting regularly in a less formal way).
- They allow time for you to discuss your progress, reflect on what you have done and set goals for the coming weeks.
- They allow your supervisor to track your work so that they will be able to authenticate your final essay.

These meetings also create space for you to think purposefully about what you are learning regarding your subject and topic, and what you are learning about yourself, such as:

- skills and experience which you can apply to other areas of study and life
- obstacles or challenges you are encountering and how you are overcoming them
- what you are doing well
- areas for growth or development.

Your supervisor will record these required meetings on your Reflection on Progress Form (RPF); these meetings will also provide material for your reflective statement.

What happens at formal meetings?

Your extended essay coordinator will give you more information on what to accomplish at each meeting and how to prepare, but the following diagrams offer some general information.

Meeting	When?	Before and during the meeting	Reflection
Initial meeting	During your initial exploration (as you are beginning the process, deciding on a research question, and so on)	**You might:** • create your RRS • begin brainstorming topics • craft a working research question • put together a research proposal • do background reading. **Your supervisor might:** • discuss the extended essay requirements with you • help you brainstorm and refine topics • ensure the feasibility of your topic (or direct you to someone who can) • ask probing questions to help you think critically about the process • help you articulate your goals for the process, the areas, traits and skills you feel confident in as well as where you seek to grow • encourage you to create a research plan and schedule.	**Before, during and immediately after, reflect in your RRS on any or all of the following questions:** • What topics am I interested in and why? • Do I know and understand the extended essay requirements, subject-specific requirements and assessment criteria for the extended essay? • Why have I chosen this subject or why might I use an interdisciplinary approach? • What do I feel are my strengths, in terms of learner profile traits (see page 6), approaches to learning (see page 7), and so on? • Which skills or traits do I think I may need to develop or strengthen and what steps can I take to set myself up for success? • What do I want to get out of this process and what are my concerns or fears? • How am I maintaining balance?
Interim meeting	During the research or writing phase	**You might:** • do background and more in-depth research • make notes in your RRS as you read • create a working, annotated bibliography • determine your research methods, approach, and any theoretical frameworks • articulate the purpose and benefits of an interdisciplinary approach (if applicable) • create a writing schedule. **Your supervisor might:** • read and discuss a piece of work you have been developing (such as initial research notes, a paragraph draft, an outline or an annotated bibliography) • provide written or oral feedback on your complete rough draft (focusing on overall elements like the structure and flow of your argument, and the use and analysis of evidence, rather than line-by-line edits or prescriptive revisions) • discuss your sources with you and recommend new or alternative sources for your research.	**Before, during and immediately after, reflect in your RRS on any or all of the following questions:** • Is my research question viable, effective and clear? • Are there any issues that have arisen since our last meeting? • Is what I have been doing effective and appropriate (in terms of research, methods, timeline, and so on)? • Do I have enough sources? • What successes have I experienced (perhaps in terms of communication or organisation skills)? • How am I learning or changing thus far in the process – both in terms of my knowledge of the subject matter and in terms of my personal growth? • How am I maintaining balance?
Viva voce (final meeting)	At the end of the process, after you have submitted your final essay	**You should:** • bring some notes you have written to help guide your reflection on the process as a whole • bring your essay and any other materials from your RRS that you might wish to refer to • think through what you have learned about your topic and subject, and how your thinking has or has not changed or developed • think through how you have grown or changed as a learner, thinker, communicator, time manager, and so on. **Your supervisor will:** • have read the final version of your essay beforehand • celebrate your success in completing the extended essay process • discuss with you what you have learned • help you think through your reflective statement.	**Before, during and immediately after, reflect in your RRS on any or all of the following questions:** • What skills, knowledge or understanding have I gained from this process? • How might I use these new skills in further study and in life outside the classroom? • What challenges or obstacles did I face? How did I learn from them? What has this taught me about myself? • What do I feel most proud of? Note: After the viva voce, you will complete your reflective statement and enter it into your RPF.

> **Remember**
> The viva voce is a short interview that follows the completion of your extended essay. It serves as a celebration of your accomplishment and provides an opportunity for reflection on what you have learned. This is not an assessment of your research or essay content, but rather a chance to reflect on your personal growth through the process. The discussion will provide valuable material for your final reflective statement.

Getting the most out of the meetings

Meetings with your supervisor are designed to help you, so here is how to get the most out of them.

Be proactive!
Most supervisors are also full-time teachers with various other responsibilities, so the earlier you contact your supervisor to arrange a meeting, the better. Be a caring communicator: ask your supervisor how they prefer to be contacted, whether by email or in person, and share your schedule with them so you can determine the best time for both of you to meet. For example, if you need to arrange one of the three formal, required meetings, contact your supervisor at least two weeks in advance. Do not worry if you are not yet ready for the meeting at this point – you just want to get on their schedule.

Help them help you!
As soon as possible, send or give your supervisor any materials they might need to read in advance of your meeting, such as draft materials, questions or an annotated bibliography. You will be able to use the time together most efficiently if your supervisor does not have to read the materials in the meeting while you wait.

Prepare!
Before the meeting, look back through your RRS and any other notes you have made to ensure that you have all your questions ready. Jot them down on a piece of paper so that you do not forget anything! Go to the meeting with materials you may need, such as your laptop, your research notes and any reflections and documents you are currently working on.

Reflect!
Take 5–10 minutes after your meeting to note down what you discussed while it is still fresh in your head, particularly any action steps or follow-up tasks you will need to complete, as well as how you are feeling about the process, what you are learning, struggling with, and so on. All these notes will help you write the most detailed and effective reflective statement at the end of the process.

The reflective statement and why it matters

The reflective statement is a 500-word reflection written at the end of the extended essay process. It is entered on the Reflection on Progress Form (RPF), which is submitted to IB along with your essay. This is where you will formally articulate what you have learned and how you have grown and changed over the extended essay process.

Your reflective statement should be evaluative rather than descriptive. You should include specific examples from your extended essay journey and demonstrate how the process has contributed to your growth and learning. Evidence in your reflection might include:

- experiences and insights that could shape your future thinking
- explicit examples of how skills learned could be used in other current contexts and in the future
- how changes in perspective impacted your decision-making.

How the reflective statement is scored

The reflective statement is formally assessed along with your essay, according to Criterion E. This means that the score you earn on your reflective statement contributes to the overall score on your extended essay.

The guiding question for Criterion E is 'Does the student evaluate the effect of the extended essay learning experience on them as a learner?' This is scored from 1–4 and focuses mainly on your ability to evaluate and analyse yourself, and to identify your growth as a result of the process. Just like your essay, your reflective statement should avoid summary and description, and focus instead on analysis and evaluation.

Do ...	Do not ...
✓ explain how you have grown and changed as a result of the process	✗ simply describe or list what you did
✓ include a few examples or evidence of that change – for example, a new understanding you experienced or an obstacle you overcame	✗ focus on the *what* rather than the *how*, *why* or *so what*
✓ identify how you might transfer your new knowledge and skills to other tasks or areas of life	✗ communicate a lack of genuine engagement with the process or your topic
✓ evaluate how your thinking evolved or changed over the process	✗ remain superficial and general in your reflection
✓ focus on the *how*, *why* and *so what* of the process.	✗ reveal a lack of self-awareness or effort in thinking through how the extended essay process affected you.

A high-scoring reflective statement will show that you are self-aware, that you can critically self-assess, and that you have engaged honestly and intentionally with the process to grow and develop as a person.

Look at the examples of reflective statements below, and the commentaries on their strengths and weaknesses.

> # Example 1
>
> My extended essay was about employee motivation at Apple Inc. I chose this topic because I'm interested in how big tech companies manage their workers and wanted to learn about different motivation theories. The process of writing the extended essay took much longer than I thought it would.
>
> First, I researched different motivation theories like Maslow's Hierarchy and Herzberg's Two-Factor Theory. I found information from business textbooks and online articles about Apple. It was hard to find specific

information about Apple's internal practices because they are really private, but I found some news articles and interviews with former employees.

Writing the essay required me to explain different theories and then apply them to Apple. I wrote about their employee benefits, work environment and leadership style. My supervisor helped me organise my ideas better and told me when I needed more evidence for my claims.

I learned about different ways companies motivate employees. The hardest part was trying to analyse Apple's practices because I couldn't find much direct information. I used examples from their company policies and public statements to support my arguments. My supervisor told me to add more analysis, so I tried to do that.

Sometimes it was difficult to meet deadlines because I had other assignments to complete. The final essay discussed Apple's motivation strategies and whether they were effective. I think the experience was useful because now I understand more about how businesses work.

Overall, writing the extended essay helped me learn about business management and improved my research skills.

This reflection is weak because it:

- simply describes what was done without meaningful reflection
- uses generic statements ('learned about different ways')
- focuses on basic tasks rather than learning insights
- provides no specific examples of personal growth
- shows no real evaluation of research methods or thinking processes
- makes superficial connections to learning ('now I understand more')
- misses opportunities to discuss how challenges shaped understanding of business research
- does not make use of the full 500 words.

Example 2

My extended essay on the environmental effects of palm oil production in Indonesia taught me a lot about scientific research. When I started, I thought it would be simple to show that palm oil was bad for the environment, but I learned that research is more complicated than that.

One of the main challenges I faced was finding good sources. At first, I only used environmental websites that talked about deforestation, but my supervisor told me I needed to use academic sources. This was hard because many of the scientific papers were difficult to understand, and I spent a lot of time looking up terms I didn't know. Eventually, I found some good journal articles that helped me understand the topic better.

I had to change my research question several times. My first question was too broad because it tried to cover too many environmental impacts. My supervisor helped me focus specifically on biodiversity loss in Borneo, which made the essay more manageable. This taught me that it is important to have a focused research question.

The writing process was challenging because I had never written such a long academic paper before. I learned how to structure an argument and use evidence to support my points. Sometimes I would make statements without backing them up with sources, but my supervisor helped me fix this. I also learned how to cite sources properly, which will be useful in university.

During my research, I found some surprising information. While palm oil production does cause deforestation, it is actually more efficient than other oil crops in terms of land use. This made me realise that environmental issues are more complex than they might seem at first. However, I still think palm oil production is a serious problem that needs to be addressed.

The hardest part was analysing the data from different studies. I mainly summarised what each study said rather than comparing them properly. My supervisor suggested I create a table to compare the findings, which helped me see patterns I hadn't noticed before. I could have done more detailed analysis, but at least I learned how to organise information better.

Looking back, I think I have improved my research skills through this process. I now know how to find academic sources and write formally. If I were to do it again, I would spend more time analysing the data and less time just describing what other researchers found. I also learned that scientific research isn't always black and white – there can be multiple perspectives on environmental issues.

This is a mid-range reflection offering some good insight, but it is also a little superficial and descriptive in places. Overall, the reflection displays some growth but often defaults to surface-level observations rather than deep analysis of the learning process.

Strengths:

- Shows some awareness of learning (recognising complexity of the issue).
- Includes specific examples of challenges faced.
- Acknowledges some weaknesses in the approach.

Weaknesses:

- Often stays at a descriptive level ('I learned ...' without deeper reflection).
- Contains vague statements ('taught me a lot').
- Lacks sophisticated analysis of how these experiences changed their thinking.
- Misses opportunities to evaluate impact on academic development.
- Limited discussion of how challenges were overcome.
- More focused on what happened than what was learned.

Example 3

My extended essay examining how local newspapers shaped public opinion during the 1919 Seattle General Strike transformed my understanding of historical research and challenged my assumptions about objectivity in journalism. What began as a straightforward analysis of newspaper coverage evolved into a complex exploration of media bias, class relations and competing narratives during a pivotal moment in labour history.

Initially, I struggled with source interpretation. My first draft simply summarised newspaper articles, treating them as factual accounts rather than pieces of historical evidence that needed contextual analysis. Through conversations with my supervisor, I learned to consider crucial questions: Who owned these newspapers? What were their political leanings? How did their portrayal of strikers differ from other contemporary accounts? This taught me that historical research requires reading both within and beyond sources.

> The most significant challenge emerged in the archives. Many newspaper issues were damaged or missing, forcing me to adapt my research approach. Rather than seeing this as an obstacle, I expanded my investigation to include personal letters and union pamphlets, which provided counterpoints to mainstream media coverage. This experience showed me how limitations can actually enrich research by necessitating a more diverse range of primary sources.
>
> My approach to historical evidence matured considerably throughout this process. Early in my research, I tended to accept anti-union newspaper characterisations at face value. However, as I developed stronger analytical skills, I began examining how word choice, article placement, and selective reporting shaped public perception. For example, discovering how different newspapers used contrasting language to describe the same events helped me understand the media's role in framing social conflicts.
>
> The writing process revealed my tendency to judge historical events from my contemporary beliefs. My supervisor helped me see where I imposed modern perspectives on 1919 attitudes. Learning to contextualise events within their historical period while maintaining analytical distance was challenging but crucial. I now understand that good historical writing requires both empathy for historical perspectives and critical analysis of them.
>
> This journey taught me that historical research is far more than gathering facts - it is about understanding how different pieces of evidence interact to create a fuller picture of the past. When I discovered contradictions between newspaper accounts and personal letters, I learned that these inconsistencies often reveal the most interesting aspects of historical events.
>
> Looking back, I see how this experience has developed my ability to think like a historian. Beyond specific research skills, I have learned to question dominant narratives, consider multiple perspectives, and understand how past events are interpreted through various lenses. The extended essay has shown me that studying history is not just about learning what happened, but understanding how we know what we know about the past.
>
> This reflection is effective for several key reasons. The student:
> - demonstrates genuine growth and learning (for example, from simple to complex understanding)
> - acknowledges initial limitations honestly and explains how they were overcome
> - explains specific moments of realisation rather than vague statements
> - uses specific examples (concrete challenges, real examples of learning moments, and so on.)
> - illustrates changes in thinking with actual instances from the research process
> - shows critical self-reflection
> - analyses mistakes (presentism, oversimplification)
> - evaluates changes in approach
> - connects specific experiences to broader learning outcomes
> - demonstrates academic maturity (for example, acknowledges complexity and nuance).
>
> Most importantly, it feels authentic rather than formulaic – it tells a genuine story of intellectual growth through specific examples while maintaining academic rigour.

Planning and writing your reflective statement

You will write your reflective statement after your viva voce. If you have been reflecting throughout the process, you should have plenty of material to work with. The reflective statement should be about 500 words, which means you have plenty of space to discuss your process, provide examples of learning moments, and analyse your growth.

Your reflective statement is personal, so you can write in the first person. However, remember that it is still a piece of formal, academic writing, so take the time to write complete sentences, edit for clarity and flow, and proofread for errors before submitting.

Activity

Practise turning a descriptive statement below into a more analytical, evaluative discussion. For example, take this statement:

I learned a lot about research methods.

Make it more specific and evaluative:

- I learned how to find academic sources.
- My approach to source evaluation evolved from simply accepting information to questioning methodology.
- A critical moment in my development as a researcher came when …

Now you try it

Choose one or more of these descriptive statements and follow the same process to make it more specific and evaluative.

Statement 1: I learned about research methods.

Statement 2: My writing improved.

Statement 3: I learned how to use primary sources.

Statement 4: I got better at analysing data.

Activity

Use a chart to record how you adapted to challenges along the way. For example:

Challenge (event)	Initial response	How I adapted	Evidence of growth
Limited access to company data for my case study on Nike's supply chain sustainability.	Relied only on public news articles and company reports.	Broadened research to include academic papers on industry practices, NGO reports, and comparative analysis with competitors.	My final analysis included multiple stakeholder perspectives, showing how different sources revealed contrasting narratives about supply chain practices.

Now you try it

As you are thinking through your own extended essay journey, create a chart like the one in the activity above in your RRS. Try to include at least three different examples or moments along your journey.

Activity

Create a visual timeline of your research process. At each key point, write:

- what happened (descriptive)
- what you thought at the time (analytical)
- how this changed your approach (evaluative)
- what you learned about yourself as a researcher (reflective).

Example of one point:

- 15 September: Initial experiment design
- What happened: Set up hydroponic systems for testing three fertiliser types
- Thoughts at time: 'This setup seems straightforward – just add different fertilisers and measure growth'
- How it changed my approach: After two failed trials, realised environmental controls were crucial
- Learning as researcher: Initially underestimated complexity of controlling variables; discovered importance of detailed experimental protocols

Now you try it

In your RRS, create a visual timeline of your own research process, including statements that are:

- descriptive
- analytical
- evaluative
- reflective.

Remember

Use words like 'realised', 'transformed', 'challenged', 'reconsidered' and 'developed' as you are discussing your process. These will lead you at least to the beginning of an evaluative statement!

Key takeaways: Chapter 12

- There are three required supervisor meetings, but it is useful to have other, informal check-ins with your supervisor.
- Be proactive with supervisor meetings – schedule early, come prepared, and follow up with notes.
- The reflective statement (500 words) is assessed under Criterion E and should show your growth as a learner.
- In your reflective statement, focus on evaluation over description – explain how and why your thinking changed, not just what you did.
- Document your journey in your RRS to help write a stronger reflective statement later.

Key term

viva voce: (Latin 'with living voice') the final session or 'interview' with your extended essay supervisor – an oral defence of the extended essay, which also includes discussion and reflection on the process as a whole and what has been learned, personally and about the topic

Chapter 13 – The whole you: coming full circle

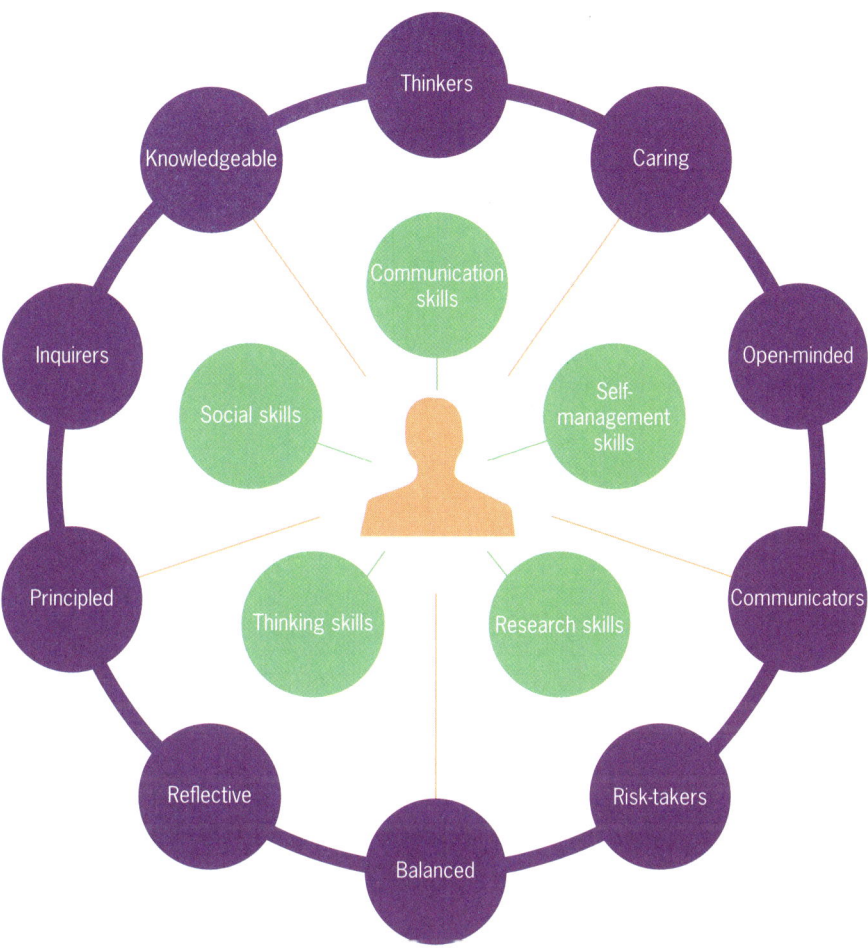

Congratulations on completing the IB extended essay! This is a remarkable achievement, and one that has hopefully helped you grow and develop as both a scholar and a person.

Celebrate your success and remember to take the skills and knowledge you have gained in this process into other areas of life, study and future endeavours. Not only will they help you in your DP courses and assessments, they will also make you a stronger candidate for higher education and employment. After all, you can now explain and capitalise on those approaches to learning skills:

- Communication (such as writing and speaking)
- Thinking (such as data analysis and synthesis)
- Research (such as media literacy and ethical scholarship)
- Social interactions (such as increased empathy and confidence when working with mentors)
- Self-management (such as organisation, time management, emotional resilience, and self-awareness)

You can also demonstrate how you embody the learner profile traits that make you an ideal member of any academic or professional community. Thanks to your hard work in the extended essay process, you understand how to call on these traits and roles in various contexts and situations:

- Caring
- Open-minded
- Principled
- Balanced
- Knowledgeable
- Reflective
- Thinker
- Inquirer
- Risk-taker
- Communicator

Most importantly, carry with you the spirit of inquiry that fuelled your extended essay journey. The curiosity that drove you to ask meaningful questions, seek out diverse perspectives, and persist through challenges is a powerful tool that will serve you well, whether you are tackling university coursework, engaging in global conversations, or shaping your own career path. Wherever life takes you, let this experience remind you that you have the skills, mindset and resilience to meet new challenges with confidence and curiosity.

Well done – and best of luck in all your future endeavours!

Glossary

abstract: a summary of the contents of a piece of academic research

action verbs: verbs that describe the action that the subject of a sentence performs

AI tools: software that uses artificial intelligence algorithms to solve problems and perform tasks

analysis: the process of considering something carefully or using statistical methods in order to understand or explain it

artefact: an object made by human work

canonical: describing something that belongs to an officially recognised group of writings

cite: to refer and give credit to someone else's work

conceptual understanding: a deep comprehension of key ideas, principles and theories, which allows you to make connections across disciplines and apply knowledge to new contexts, rather than merely memorising facts

connotation: an association or idea suggested by a word or phrase

context: the parts of a piece of writing, speech, and so on, that precede and follow a word or passage and contribute to its full meaning; the circumstances in which something occurs or exists

contextualisation: placing an idea within its relevant background or framework, showing how it fits into the larger picture

conventions: agreed-upon rules for writing (such as grammar, punctuation, formatting and spelling)

counter-argument: a set of reasons set forward to oppose or disprove an idea that has been developed in another argument

data: a collection or series of facts, observations or measurements, often presented in the form of numbers or letters

DOI: Digital Object Identifier; a unique string of numbers, letters, and symbols assigned to digital content (such as online articles) which provides a permanent link to their location on the internet (since URLs can change or expire)

edit: to correct errors and improve clarity at the sentence level (such as grammar, spelling and formatting)

empirical: based on observation and experience rather than on theory

ethical: relating to rules or conduct and beliefs about what is morally right or wrong

evaluation: the process of assessing or judging the quality or importance of something

expository: a piece of writing that offers an explanation or narration of something

fieldwork: investigations or search for material or data in a real, natural environment rather than in school, work or laboratory

footnotes: notes printed at the bottom of a page that provide extra information, explanation or references about something that has been mentioned on that page

framework: the essential concepts, theories and approaches that underpin a subject of study

hypothesis: a suggested explanation for a group of facts or phenomena, which is accepted as likely to be true

index: an alphabetised list, found at the end of a book, of key terms, ideas, names and topics covered within that book, along with page numbers where each can be found within the text

informed consent: permission given by someone who understands fully what they are agreeing to

integrate: to meaningfully combine and synthesise concepts, methodologies and insights from two subjects

interdisciplinary: combining more than one academic subject to examine topics or solve problems

jargon: specialised language concerned within a particular subject, culture or profession

metacognition: the process of thinking about one's own mental processes

method: a specific procedure, technique or way of doing something (the 'what' and 'how' of the research project); this is distinct from methodology, which is the general reasoning behind the methods chosen and the overarching approach (the 'why')

methodology: the research approaches, frameworks, and strategies used in a particular discipline

mind map: a diagram that visually represents ideas, using a central idea, with associated ideas ranged around it, connected by lines

mnemonic: a learning technique to help you remember important elements, often by creating an acronym (an abbreviation using the first letter of each word)

moral: relating to personal beliefs about what is right and wrong

parenthetical: referring to something that is written or said in addition to the main part of what you are saying, or information found inside a set of parentheses such as an in-text citation

perspective: a particular way of thinking about something, especially one that is influenced by someone's own beliefs or experiences

plagiarise: the act of using someone else's words or ideas and not crediting them

primary source: an original, first-hand or contemporary account of an event or subject

proofread: to check a piece of writing before submission, looking for any remaining errors or typos

propaganda: the purposeful distribution of information to help or harm the cause of a government or organisation

public discourse: the formal or informal exchange of ideas and arguments on issues that affect society, often in public forums, such as media and debates

qualitative analysis: an analysis based on non-quantifiable data, such as experiences or behaviour

quantitative analysis: an analysis that uses maths and statistics, considering different sizes and amounts

raw data: data that has not been processed, changed or analysed in any way (also known as primary data)

recursive: cyclical (rather than linear) structure, in which you return to different stages of the task (such as researching or writing) throughout the process

revise: to rethink and restructure content at a broader level (reorganise ideas, strengthen arguments, and so on.)

rhetorical question: a question designed to make a point rather than to get an answer

scholarly: work that is formal, sophisticated and methodical, and usually involves research and critical thinking

secondary source: a source that gives information about or analysis of a primary source, created by someone who did not experience an event first-hand

self-management skills: skills that help you take control of your own learning, behaviour and processes, such as time management, motivation, making informed choices, and so on

subject group: one of the six IB Diploma Programme subject categories, Language A (Group 1), Language B (Group 2), Individuals and Societies (Group 3), Sciences (Group 4), Mathematics (Group 5) and The Arts (Group 6)

survey: a way of gathering information by asking people a series of specific questions

synonym: a word or expression that means the same as another word or expression

synthesise: to combine separate elements into a whole

theory: a formal statement of ideas that explains an observation

thesis: a subject for a discussion or essay

topic sentence: the main sentence in a paragraph that presents the central idea of that paragraph

variable: a factor that can change in quantity, quality or size, which must be taken into consideration in a situation

Venn diagram: a diagram that uses overlapping circles to show the separate and shared features of two or more sets of information

viva voce: (Latin 'with living voice') the final session or 'interview' with your extended essay supervisor – an oral defence of the extended essay, which also includes discussion and reflection on the process as a whole and what has been learned, personally and about the topic